"Give Me That Old-Time Religion!"

Dr. John N. Hamblin

Copyright © 2010 by Berean Publications

All rights reserved. No part of this book may be reproduced or transmitted in any form or by any means without permission in writing from the publisher.

Published in Fleming Island, Florida, by Berean Publications.

Please pardon our grammar as this book was derived from sermons preached by Dr. John Hamblin and later edited by Berean Publications. Some grammar rules were overlooked due to keeping the integrity of the meaning of the sermon.

All Scripture is taken from the King James Bible.

ISBN 978-0-9771829-7-8

Printed and Bound in the United States of America

"Give Me That Old-Time Religion!"

Dr. John N. Hamblin

A Collection of Sermons

BEREAN PUBLICATIONS

A Ministry of Berean Baptist Church
4459 US Highway 17
Fleming Island, FL 32003
Phone: (904) 264-5333
Fax: (904) 264-9185
Email: info@bereanmail.org
www.thebereanbaptistchurch.com

Dedication

This bound volume of messages is dedicated to the memory and ministry of those great men of God who immeasurably impacted and inflluenced my life for the Old-Time Religion. I will forever be grateful for Dr. Tom Malone, Sr. (my beloved mentor), Dr. Curtis Hutson, Dr. Jack Hyles, Evangelist Oliver B. Greene, Evangelist Lester Roloff, Dr. B. R. Lakin, Dr. Maze Jackson, Dr. Carl Hatch, and Pastor Howard L. Woodby who called and challenged me to travel down the "Old Paths." (Jeremiah 6:16) By way of their fiery preaching, sweet fellowship, telling confidence, daily radio broadcasts, informative books, and kind personal exchanges, militant fundamentalism was birthed in my heart and a meaningful framework was built for my ministry. To each of these giants in my life, I once more pause to place a mental wreath upon their grave and take another moment to say, "Thank you for protecting and passing down to me the Old-Time Religion."

Dr. John N. Hamblin
Penned at 3:49 a.m. MST on April 27, 2010
while holding a revival meeting at the
Calvary Baptist Church in Riverton, Wyoming

Table of Contents

Foreword 9

Preface 11

Cutting Off the Voice of God 13

Does Any Christian Have a Tear? 25

Does the Devil Know You? 39

Stay on Straight Street 49

My Three Fears as a Fundamentalist 63

When God Gets in a Killing Mood 77

Please, Let Me Preach Your Funeral 87

What the Old-Time Religion Will Do for You 101

And There Arose Another Generation 113

The Most Important Piece of Furniture in the Church 127

When Senselessness Gets Sensible 137

Soulwinning 101 147

The Person in the Shadows 155

My Name is Stephanas and I am an Addict 169

What My Elijah Taught Me 183

The Synagogue of Satan 193

Foreword

Dr. John Hamblin is many things: college professor, evangelist, author. Above all, he is a preacher, but not just any kind of preacher. He is an old-fashioned, leather-lunged, independent, fundamental, KJV, sin-exposing, Devil-fighting, God-loving, evil-hating Baptist Preacher. Dr. Hamblin walks in the Old Paths, preaches the Old Book, and sees God work in Old-Time Power. He is eminently well-qualified to be a spokesman for the Old-Time Religion.

For more than a quarter of a century, Dr. Hamblin has been criss-crossing our country, opening the Word of God and unashamedly declaring its truth. His sermons are Bible-based and always have clear, direct application to the lives of the listeners.

In an age of compromise, Dr. Hamblin refuses to cut corners. Amidst a whirlwind of new ideas, he refuses to be blown off course. While "experts" are telling us that our methods are archaic, our Bible is outdated, and our standards are legalistic, Dr. Hamblin demonstrates convincingly that Spirit-empowered preaching of the Old-Time Religion still produces revival, that old-fashioned door-knocking still results in old-fashioned conversions, and that the Old Paths still bring us out to the right place.

The Gospel is still the power of God unto salvation, the Holy Spirit still convicts men of sin, the Bible is still the living Word of God. The trouble is not that the old methods are not working; the trouble is that in too many places, the old methods are not being put to work.

The messages you will read in this book have been used of God to convict sinners, comfort the struggling, confront the scorner, correct

"Give Me That Old-Time Religion!"

the saints, combat Satan, and condemn sins. Your heart will be stirred, your conscience will be pricked, your spirit will be lifted, and your soul will be blessed.

America became a great nation because of this kind of preaching. May God use these words from His faithful servant to revive His nation and draw us back to Himself.

                        Dr. R. B. Ouellette
                        Pastor First Baptist Church
                        Bridgeport, Michigan

Preface

The critics of Biblical Christianity would have us believe that the "Old-Time Religion" is an outdated slogan that has no place in our modern world. We thank God that in every generation, God will raise up faithful, uncompromising men, such as Dr. John Hamblin, to remind us that the "Old-Time Religion" will never die. The "Old-Time Religion" is the embodiment of all that we believe and stand for as believers. I am happy to recommend this book to all of those who love the "Old-Time Religion" and treasure its place in our history.

    Dr. Tom Neal
    Pastor
    Berean Baptist Church
    Fleming Island, Florida

Chapter One

Cutting Off the Voice of God

This message has weighed heavily on my heart. I am sure that a preacher can say that about every message he preaches. However, in recent days, the truth of this sermon has been a great weight upon my person. Mark 6:21-29 says, *And when a convenient day was come, that Herod on his birthday made a supper to his lords, high captains, and chief estates of Galilee; And when the daughter of the said Herodias came in, and danced, and pleased Herod and them that sat with him, the king said unto the damsel, Ask of me whatsoever thou wilt, and I will give it thee. And he sware unto her, Whatsoever thou shalt ask of me, I will give it thee, unto the half of my kingdom. And she went forth, and said unto her mother, What shall I ask? And she said, The head of John the Baptist. And she came in straightway with haste unto the king, and asked, saying, I will that thou give me by and by in a charger the head of John the Baptist. And the king was exceeding sorry; yet for his oath's sake, and for their sakes which sat with him, he would not reject her. And immediately the king sent an executioner, and commanded his head to be brought: and he went and beheaded him in the prison, And brought his head in a charger, and gave it to the damsel: and the damsel gave it to her mother. And when his disciples heard of it, they came and took up his corpse, and laid it in a tomb.*

"Give Me That Old-Time Religion!"

The verse I would like to emphasize is verse 27: *And immediately the king sent an executioner, and commanded his head to be brought: and he went and beheaded him in the prison.* The voice of God is an extremely fragile sound. It can be ignored, drowned out, and even severed. Every unbeliever and believer who has silenced this sound has lived to regret it. It would be worlds better for a man to never hear the song of a bird, the laughter of a baby, or the rippling of a brook than to never hear the still, small voice of Deity. In Mark Chapter 6, we find the twelve sent out, John the Baptist beheaded, and the apostles returned. Its entire theme is the triumphs and tragedies in Galilee. The nine verses that are before us deal with a tragedy. John the Baptist was beheaded. This chapter can be easily outlined or laid out like this:

    Verse 21 - Herod's Party
    Verse 22 - Herod's Pleasure
    Verse 23 - Herod's Promise
    Verses 24-25 - Herod's Painted Lady
    Verse 26 - Herod's Pride
    Verses 27-29 - Herod's Prisoner

It is while the Apostle Mark is dealing under the direct inspiration of the Holy Spirit about Herod's prisoner, that he pens one of the most stirring verses in Scripture. It is not only the most stirring, but also the saddest. Verse 27 says, *And immediately the king sent an executioner, and commanded his head to be brought: and he went and beheaded him in the prison.* The even more sorrowful sister verse of Mark 6:27 would have to be Luke 23:9. The Bible says, *Then he [Herod] questioned with him [Christ] in many words; but he [Christ] answered him [Herod] nothing.* Herein lies Herod's horrible result for having the head of John the Baptist hacked off. When the Lord Jesus Christ stands before him on the way to Calvary, a deafening answer of silence rings in the ears of Herod to every single question he submits to the Son of God. He is the only sinner to whom the Saviour refused to speak in all of the four Gospels. The sovereign was not going to hear a word from the Saviour after he had the head of the servant put on a platter. Never forget, it

Cutting Off the Voice of God

> *Never forget, it is possible for both the unbeliever and the believer to get into a position where they have silenced God's speaking to their person.*

is possible for both the unbeliever and the believer to get into a position where they have silenced God's speaking to their person. Again I say, it is possible, and even probable, that both the unbeliever and the believer can get into a position where they silence God's speaking to their person. Friend, those of us who are saved can be committing certain sins that will always sever God's wonderful voice to our souls. I never want to get to the point that I have silenced the voice of God in my life. I am not being harsh. God knows my heart, but I believe our fundamental, independent, Bible-believing, Bible-preaching, premillennial, missionary-minded, soulwinning, temperamental Baptist churches have in them people who are just as saved as I am, but who have silenced the sound of Heaven in their souls. There are three iniquities that will always cut off God's voice to a believer.

I. Skip the Church

Hebrews 10:25 says, *Not forsaking the assembling of ourselves together, as the manner of some is; but exhorting one another: and so much the more, as ye see the day approaching.* When the believer skips the church, he will cut off God's wonderful voice to his soul. In Hebrews 10:25, the Apostle Paul tells us that the Christian is to make sure that he attends church services and is even to add more church services in his life as he senses that he is drawing closer to Christ's Second Coming. As the newspaper, television, and radio reports, these are the days of apostasy, apathy, and even anarchy. So, the child of God should not be trying to subtract church services but should be trying to add church services to his weekly schedule. When one-time fundamentalists are calling the last pope one of the greatest moral and spiritual leaders in our century, when churches get bigger crowds for a sporting event than a soulwinning evening, and when one almost fears for his life when he is pumping gas at his neighborhood gas station, it is thirty minutes past

"Give Me That Old-Time Religion!"

time to beat it down to the house of God. Friend, we are cutting off the voice of God when we skip the church.

The Bible says in II Peter 3:18, *But grow in grace, and in the knowledge of our Lord and Saviour Jesus Christ.* When we fly the coop when it comes to the church, in a real sense, we are doing the very same thing that Herod did to John the Baptist. The Christian's growth and his church attendance are closely connected. I can prove that without question and without controversy. Just think about a Christian who is growing in grace. Without any debate or discussion, it has to be determined that a Christian must be connected to the church. No one ever grows, glows, or goes for God unless he or she is connected to the church. Now, with that truth firmly fixed in all of our minds, there is no sense in beating around the bush when it comes to this matter of being faithful to all the church services. We are fooling ourselves if we think we are going to grow spiritually and stay in bed under the covers during Sunday school. "Bedside Baptist" has never had a good Sunday school program. Never has! A person does not go to a good Sunday school program when he is at "Bedside Baptist." They just do not have it. The reason that some folks do not go to Sunday school can be plainly put. It is mind over mattress. That is the reason they do not go. Now, I have to be really honest. I am an evangelist, and I know that it was not an evangelist who created and crafted Sunday school. Most of the time, either Saturday night and even Sunday morning, we are still traveling from point A to point B to have a service at 10 o'clock, after we have gotten in late at night or even early in the morning. Ten o'clock tends to get on one's nerves. So, I know that it was not an evangelist who created Sunday school; nonetheless, we are fooling ourselves when we think we can have Sunday school at "Bedside Baptist" and grow spiritually.

We are kidding ourselves if we think we are going to grow spiritually when we only come to Sunday morning services on Christmas and Easter. Recently, I noticed a sign as I was parking in a church's parking lot that said, "Always Open." I like that. I think there are people who are members of fundamental churches who need to find out that we are open between Easter and Christmas. We are always open. When some people show up, we automatically think, "Oh no, I haven't got my stocking stuffers! Oh no! I haven't gotten my wife a Christmas poinsettia or Easter lily. I haven't hidden any Easter eggs yet. Oh no! It must be a holiday."

We are bamboozling ourselves if we think we are going to grow spiritually and let what is on television on Sunday night be more important than what is on the preacher's heart. People who know what is on television on Sunday nights and Wednesday nights are not very good church members. I have no clue what is on television on Sunday night. If somebody were to put a gun to my head and say, "Tell me what's on television Sunday night, or I'll pull the trigger," I will pull the trigger for him. I have no idea what is on television on Sunday night and Wednesday night. I am just under the conviction that a good church member has no clue or concept of what is on the "idot box" on Sunday and Wednesday nights. We are hoodwinking ourselves if we think we are going to grow spiritually when we choose to work overtime during the mid-week service.

And, last but by no means least of all, we are deceiving ourselves if we think we are going to grow spiritually when we purposely plan other things when our church is in revival meeting. Recently, I was preaching two nights at a conference. I was the second preacher. I walked in to preach the first night of that conference literally having gotten off a plane, going from one pulpit to the next. As I walked in, the first preacher was already preaching. When they broke between the two preachers, a lady who happened to be the church pianist walked up to me and said, "I sure hope you appreciate my cancelling my Tupperware party to be in this meeting." My dear friend, we need revival. We need revival in a desperate way when people think it is a sacrifice to cancel a stupid Tupperware party for a revival meeting at the house of God. We are absolutely deceiving ourselves if we think we are going to grow spiritually when we purposely plan other things when our church is in a revival meeting.

I like what I read years ago on a small country church sign. This sign could be read from the road. Under the times of services and the address of the church was written, "Visitors welcomed, but members expected." I believe that is the way God feels about it, "Visitors welcomed, but members expected." Someone once asked an elderly lady

"Give Me That Old-Time Religion!"

about her son-in-law's church attendance. "Is he a church member?" he wondered.

"Well, yes." said the old lady hesitantly. "At least he is a trunk member." When asked for an explanation, the lady replied, "Well, that's what I have always called those church members who join a church and then put their membership letter at the bottom of a trunk. There it lies whether it gets moved about or stays in one place for thirty years. They seldom go to church. They take little or no part in the service. They contribute irregularly, if at all. They are not active members working for the Lord. They are just trunk members." Hey, Christian, do not be a trunk member and cut off the voice of God.

II. Snub the Preacher

Romans 10:14 says, *How then shall they call on him in whom they have not believed? and how shall they believe in him of whom they have not heard? and how shall they hear without a preacher?* When the believer snubs the preacher, he cuts off God's wonderful voice to his soul. In Romans 10:14, the Apostle Paul tells us that people, whether they are unbelievers or believers, need to hearken and hear the truth. There must be, at some point or some place, a heralder, one who delivers the message of truth, placed in their paths. Friend, for an unbeliever or a believer to hearken unto truth, there must be a heralder at some point in some place, put in his or her path who heralds truth. When we cold-shoulder a preacher, in a real sense, we are doing the same thing that Herod did to John the Baptist. Friend, when we snub the preacher, we cut off the voice of God. Now, there are several practical things that a Christian can do to keep from ignoring God's man.

The first practical thing that a Christian can do to keep from ignoring God's man is concentrate on his message. Revelation 2:7 says, *He that hath an ear, let him hear what the Spirit saith unto the churches...* Every ear should be tuned in to what the minister is saying when he is standing behind the sacred pulpit, because this is the way that the Holy Spirit deliberately speaks to the members. Now, we are not going to do it; but if we were to put someone at the door, and say, "You will not go home unless you can give one of the three points that Dr. John Hamblin preached tonight," would we go home?

When our children were much smaller Mrs. Hamblin would ask, "Now, what did Dad preach?" And they would say, "Well, Dad preached the Bible." or "Dad preached about Jesus." When they got a little bit older, they would say, "Dad preached on the platform. That's what Dad preached on." And then as they got older yet, they would say, "Dad preached on modernism, and Dad preached on liberalism." They would ask, "Now, are we going to get a gold star because we told Mom that Dad preached on modernism and on liberalism?" Hey, Dad always preaches on modernism and liberalism!

Can anybody tell me what his or her pastor preached last Wednesday night? It is a shame, a tragedy, and even a sin when we do not concentrate on a preacher's message. Because we do not concentrate, we end up ignoring the man of God. Concentrate on the preacher's message!

The second practical thing that a Christian can do to keep from ignoring God's man is to consider his advice. Proverbs 11:14 says, *Where no counsel is, the people fall: but in the multitude of counselors there is safety.* It would be impossible to even guess at the number of believers who could have been helped and the homes that could have been held together, if people would have just taken the counsel of the man of God. Now, I would be the first to admit that our counsel is not perfect. But on the heels of that, let me hasten to say that one will never get counsel that has more of the Bible in mind and more of our best interest in mind than from a man of God. Though it may not always be perfectly conveyed, it will be from the Bible. Though it may not be perfect, it will be in a person's spiritual best interest; and it sure beats counsel one can get over a fence, over a pew, or over the internet. It beats all that kind of counsel by far. Consider a preacher's advice.

> *It would be impossible to even guess at the number of believers who could have been helped and the homes that could have been held together, if people would have just taken the counsel of the man of God.*

"Give Me That Old-Time Religion!"

The third practical thing that a Christian can do to keep from ignoring God's man is to count on his supplication. James 5:16b says, *The effectual fervent prayer of a righteous man availeth much.* When we face any kind of problem, peril, or predicament, we can ask a preacher in whom we have great confidence to pray for us. Count on a preacher's supplication. Oh, that every Christian would just decide that he or she is going to do the practical things to keep from ever ignoring God's man. Oh, that every Christian would concentrate on a preacher's message, consider a preacher's advice, and count on a preacher's supplication.

I read recently that there was a butcher who ran a little shop on the edge of London. He decided one Sunday to go into town to hear the great preacher, Charles Hadden Spurgeon. His wife chose not to go with him. So, the butcher went to town, went to the Metropolitan Tabernacle, and then went home. That afternoon, his wife began to question and probe him about the service. "What songs did they sing?"

He said, "I don't remember."

"Well, what was his text?"

Again he said, "I don't remember."

Somewhat exasperated, his wife wanted to know, "What good did it do for you to go to church this morning?"

The butcher was quiet for what seemed like an eternity, and finally he spoke, "What good? I will tell you what good. You know those scales out in the shop that really weigh just fourteen ounces to the pound? Well, before we open for business in the morning, I am going to correct those scales to where they weigh a full sixteen ounces to the pound." Listen, Christian, although that butcher may have been skillful with a meat cleaver, he still had enough spiritual sense to listen to Mr. Spurgeon's sermon and not cut off God's voice to his heart.

III. Sadden the Holy Ghost

Ephesians 4:30 says, *And grieve not the holy Spirit of God, whereby ye are sealed unto the day of redemption.* When the believer saddens the Holy Ghost, he cuts off God's wonderful voice to his soul. In Ephesians 4:30, the Apostle Paul tells us that it is possible for the believer to distress the Third Person of the Trinity, Who takes up His

Cutting Off the Voice of God

permanent dwelling in each person the second he gets saved. The word *grieve* is an interesting word. In the Greek language, it means "to be in heaviness or sorrow." This startling truth means that the wrong attitudes and actions of the believer cause the Holy Spirit to experience the exact same emotion that a person feels when he stands at the heart-wrenching entrance of an extremely close loved one's grave. G. Campbell Morgan, a great Bible student of yesteryear, used to say, "How would you like to live with someone who everlastingly was grieving your heart by his conduct?" In the Old Testament, the temple was a building; and in the New Testament, it is a body. That means that the very moment that we trusted Christ, the Third Person of the Trinity came in and took up permanent occupancy, and He lives in our bodies if we are saved. When we do those things that grieve Him and cause Him to sorrow, what we are really doing is cutting off the voice of God in our lives. In the Old Testament, the most sacred place was the building where God's power was. In the New Testament, the most sacred place is the body where God's power still dwells as the Spirit of God moved in the moment we got saved. That means we are tabernacles. That means we are the dwelling places of the Spirit of God. That means we are temples. Friend, we cut off the voice of God when we sadden the Holy Ghost.

Mark 1:10 states in one of the most important verses for the believer, layman or a preacher, *And straightway coming up out of the water, he saw the heavens opened, and the Spirit like a dove descending upon him.* Someone might say, "That's a big statement: 'One of the most important verses for a layman or a preacher.'" Oh, yes! When we break the heart of the Holy Ghost, in a real sense, we are doing the very same thing that Herod did to John the Baptist. In Mark 1:10, the Holy Ghost is typified and pictured as a dove. When the Son of God was baptized, the Spirit of God descended upon Him in the form of a dove. It is intriguing that the dove, the bird that is the most easily startled and most easily scared of all birds, was chosen to picture the work of the paraclete. It was not an owl, a robin, or an eagle, but a dove that was picked to picture the work of a paraclete. News flash: A Christian's strange beliefs and sinful behaviors will always startle and scare the Heavenly Dove.

"Give Me That Old-Time Religion!"

Now, may I bring it down to where we live? It is not so much wrong actions, but wrong attitudes. It is not so much strange beliefs, but sinful behaviors. Our problem is not that we are in a tattoo parlor, a saloon, a bar, or a tavern. Our problem is not that we are in a drug den or house of ill repute. Our problem is that we are in the house of God with the wrong mindset. Primarily, our problem is not wrong actions, but it is wrong attitudes. Because of wrong attitudes, we grieve that Dove. By the way, we got the Dove the moment that we asked Jesus to save us. That Dove moved in and took up permanent occupancy in our body. I just thought of it; we are a birdcage! We are a spiritual birdcage for the Holy Spirit. So, our problem is not wrong actions but wrong attitudes.

To illustrate, someone might say, "Well, I don't know why we would have a revival meeting just before Christmas?" That is a wrong attitude. "Well, I don't know why these people are not here. Why, they need this more than I do." That is the wrong attitude. "Why does Dr. John Hamblin have to scream, spit, and sweat, but let me hasten to say, look sharp?" That is the wrong attitude. The Holy Spirit is startled in our lives.

I was reading recently that there was a guide in the deserts of Arabia who had never lost his way. He had that reputation. He never lost his way because he always carried with him a homing pigeon. The homing pigeon had a cord that was tied to its leg and then tied to a button of the guide. Whenever the guide did not know where he was, he would take out that homing pigeon and release it. It would soar to the sky, find its direction, and head toward home. Because of that practice, that guide was given the nickname, *Dove Man*, by all the other guides. He was given the moniker, *Dove Man*. Every one of us has a Dove with us all the time. He walks with me, talks with me, and shows me life's way. Every one of us has the Heavenly Dove with us all the time. Many times, it is not so much our actions as it is our attitudes that startle and make scared the Dove in our lives. We say things that have wounded the Dove. We think things that have wounded the Dove.

A couple of weeks back, I was going through security in the Philadelphia airport. I do not know why it is, but I always get pulled out of line at the security checkpoint. If I fit the profile of a terrorist, I am in trouble. Every time, I get jerked aside and searched. I do not even have a diaper on my head, but those who do just go right through security. Going through security is always an uptight and tense time because I know that surely I am going to get pulled aside and searched. Of course, they will not find anything; but it is just a real pain in the neck. So, I was going through security; and my cell phone rang. I answered it, and it was Mrs. Hamblin. She said, "Hey, Babe, what are you doing?"

I said, "Well, I'm going through security."

"Well, I won't keep you. When you get through security, let me know."

Just as I was stepping through security the light went off, the horn blew, and the security guards came from every direction. I told my wife, "Well, I'll call you right back." I was a little short with her when I hung up. Of course, they pulled me aside; and I said, "Wait a minute. I need to do something."

They asked me, "What do you need to do?"

I said, "I need to make a call. You may search me, but I need to do this first." I called my wife right back. I said, "Hey, I was a little bit short with you. I'm sorry. I'll call you in a minute."

She said, "That's all right. I heard the alarms and knew you were going through security. No problem."

I said, "No, it is a problem because the Spirit of God convicted me." Now, I did not cuss or say a bad word; but I was a little bit tart, a little bit short. Just as soon as it happened, that Dove that we carry with us, got startled and a little bit scared in my life, and I did not want that to happen. It is not so much wrong actions, but wrong attitudes that grieve that One Who is with us all the time.

I believe we can have revival when we become sensitive to little sins. Someone may say, "Well, I would be convicted about murder." There is a whole lot of sin between here and murder. "Well, I would get convicted if I robbed a bank." That is wonderful, but there is a whole lot of sin between here and robbing a bank. "Well, I would be convicted for having another man's wife or another woman's husband." Congratulations! God bless you! But there is a whole lot between here and adultery. If we are not going to be convicted about the little stuff,

"Give Me That Old-Time Religion!"

it is highly unlikely that we will be convicted about the big stuff. They called the guide, *Dove Man*. When we are saved, the Spirit of God is with us, and we carry the Dove with us all the time. When we sadden the Holy Ghost, we cut off the voice of God to our soul. Herod had the head of John the Baptist cut off. Jesus stood before Herod. Herod asked Him a number of questions, and Jesus said nothing. What a stirring thing: Jesus said nothing. Those who are hyper-Calvinists would interpret that to mean that Herod was not saved. Of course, hyper-Calvinists interpret the Bible like Jehovah Witnesses do—wrongly. It was not that Herod could not have been saved; it was that Herod had already cut off the voice of God when he had John the Baptist's head cut off. He was an unbeliever. But I am afraid that there are believers, people just as saved as I am, who, every time the doors are open, have their hair just right, and their hems just right; but their hearts are not right. Because their hearts are not right, they are cutting off the voice of God. They are doing the very same thing, in a sense, that Herod did to John the Baptist.

Chapter Two

Does Any Christian Have a Tear?

Jeremiah 9:1-3 says, *Oh that my head were waters, and mine eyes a fountain of tears, that I might weep day and night for the slain of the daughter of my people! Oh that I had in the wilderness a lodging place of wayfaring men; that I might leave my people, and go from them! for they be all adulterers, an assembly of treacherous men. And they bend their tongues like their bow for lies: but they are not valiant for the truth upon the earth; for they proceed from evil to evil, and they know not me, saith the LORD.* I cannot read this third verse without making some type of comment. I have underscored in my Bible the statement, *but they are not valiant for the truth upon the earth...* I am not being morbid, but if Jesus stays His coming, and I go the way of all flesh, I pray that someone might be able to place upon my headstone the epitaph, "Brother Hamblin was *valiant for the truth upon the earth.*"

Verses 4-8 state, *Take ye heed every one of his neighbour, and trust ye not in any brother: for every brother will utterly supplant, and every neighbour will walk with slanders. And they will deceive every one his neighbour, and will not speak the truth: they have taught their tongue to speak lies, and weary themselves to commit iniquity. Thine habitation is in the midst of deceit; through deceit they refuse to know me, saith the LORD. Therefore thus saith the LORD of hosts, Behold, I will melt them, and try them; for how shall I do for the daughter of my people? Their tongue is as an arrow shot out; it speaketh deceit: one speaketh peaceably to his neighbour with his mouth, but in heart he layeth his wait.*

The verse I would like to emphasis is verse 1: *Oh that my head were waters, and mine eyes a fountain of tears, that I might weep day and night for the slain of the daughter of my people!* Does any Christian have a tear for the condition of this country? Even though America has much to cause the believer to be glad, she has almost slid to the place where there is more to cause the believer to be grieved. Breathtaking landscapes, boundless historical landmarks, and bygone bigger-than-life leaders cannot cover up the wickedness that runs rampant from the White House all the way to the poor house. The greater tragedy is that the average child of God is nowhere near an altar, weeping over a wayward nation that is on a speedboat heading straight to the rocks of God's sure judgment. Does any Christian have a tear for the condition of this country?

In Jeremiah Chapter 9, we find the prophet Jeremiah's lament for Judah. I believe that a person could go to Jeremiah Chapter 9 and literally wring out the 26 verses in this chapter and find enough tears that would literally run to the top of a tub. This chapter can be easily outlined or laid out like this:

   Verse 1 - The Sobs
   Verses 2-14 - The Sins
   Verses 15-20 - The Sufferings
   Verses 21-22 - The Steps
   Verses 23-24 - The Statements
   Verses 25-26 - The Spankings

It is while the prophet Jeremiah is dealing under the direct inspiration of the Holy Spirit that a person sees the pathos of a prophet of God for a prodigal nation in the sobs of Jeremiah. Verse 1 says, *Oh that my head were waters, and mine eyes a fountain of tears, that I might weep day and night for the slain of the daughter of my people!* Please note that it is from this particular passage of Scripture that Jeremiah would forever bear the moniker *The Weeping Prophet.* There are many events, episodes, and experiences on the pages of the Old and New Testaments where an individual, whether it be a prophet, a person, or a preacher will gain an alias, a moniker, or a nickname. From here on out, Jeremiah will be referenced and referred to as *The Weeping Prophet.*

Mark it down, there never has been the demise of a nation that brings the decline of a church, but the decline of a church that brings the demise of a nation. This thought bears repeating. It never has been the demise of a nation that brings the decline of a church, but the decline of a church that brings the demise of a nation. If an individual should doubt the accuracy of that statement, he need only read two verses in this same chapter. They are verses 25 and 26. There the Bible says, *Behold, the days come, saith the LORD, that I will punish all them which are circumcised with the uncircumcised; Egypt, and Judah, and Edom, and the children of Ammon, and Moab, and all that are in the utmost corners, that dwell in the wilderness: for all these nations are uncircumcised, and all the house of Israel are uncircumcised in the heart.* The prophet Jeremiah's brokenness is not so much over a backslidden capital as much as it was over a backslidden church. Often, when preaching this chapter, we will say that we ought to weep over America because of the saloons, and certainly, we should; or that we should weep over America because of the abortion clinics, and certainly, we should. A number of years ago, I saw a bumper sticker that put it plainly, "The mother's womb is the most dangerous place to be in America." We have preached this chapter and said that we should weep over America because of the houses of ill repute, and certainly, we should. But, when looking closely at this chapter, we see that Jeremiah was not weeping over a backslidden capital, but over a backslidden church. It is much easier to weep for what goes on outside of the church than for what goes on inside of the church. It is much easier to weep for what goes on outside of the church, and even inside of the church, than it is to weep for what goes on inside of the soul, the life, and the heart of the child of God. So, even though I have preached it this way, Jeremiah is not weeping over a capital that is wrong with God, but over a church or a group of believers that are wrong with God. Friend, we need to look past our country and look plainly at our churches and weep for its disastrous shape. Let me give three distinct places that the believer should cry over because of its disastrous shape.

I. The Pulpit That Has Lost Its Trumpet

Isaiah 58:1 says, *Cry aloud, spare not, lift up thy voice like a trumpet, and shew my people their transgression, and the house of Jacob their sins.* A distinct place that the believer should cry over because of the disastrous shape that it is in is the pulpit that has lost its trumpet. In Isaiah 58:1, the prophet Isaiah tells us about his personal and private ordination service. By the way, this is the one that the preacher must first have with Heaven before he has the other one with humans. I am not against ordination services. I preach in them all the time. But, if I had to choose between an ordination service with man or an ordination service with the Master, there would be absolutely no choice because the one that I would choose is the one with Heaven rather than the one with man.

Here is Isaiah's personal and private ordination service. It is at this time that the thrice Holy God puts His divine finger on His nose and says, "Preach!" It is absolutely amazing that, out of all the instruments in God's orchestra, He does not reach in and present the prophet with a harp, a dulcimer, a flute, a piano, an organ, a tambourine, a mandolin, an acoustic guitar, a bass guitar, a banjo, a kettle drum, or a kazoo, but a trumpet. He tells Isaiah that every time that he stands behind a sacred desk that is exactly what he is supposed to sound like.

Charles Spurgeon once said, "As God is my witness, I've eschewed every idea of trying to be eloquent or oratorical in my preaching." He went on to say, "I care nothing whatever about the gaudy show of speech making. I only want just to tell you these truths, these truths in unvarnished speech." Friend, we ought to weep, get a burden, and cry over our country when the pulpit has lost its trumpet.

The Bible says in Titus 1:13, *This witness is true. Wherefore rebuke them sharply, that they may be sound in the faith.* The main job of the fundamental pulpit is to serve as God's blaring megaphone on earth. This can never be done as long as the preacher is worried and

Does Any Christian Have a Tear?

> *The main job of the fundamental pulpit is to serve as God's blaring megaphone on earth.*

wondering what Brother Big Giver is going to do and what Sister Ratchet-jaw is going to say. Would to God, as men of God, we get back to preaching, proclaiming, and publishing the Word of God. We ought to have a burden, a tear, and a brokenness when the pulpit has lost its trumpet.

Now, if someone should wonder whether or not my concern is legitimate or whether or not my consternation is accurate, he should ask himself the question, "When was the last time that I have listened to a sermon like the sermons the great men of God have preached who are now in the Pearly City?" Here are some of the titles of the messages that preachers have preached who now are in Heaven: "Hot Cakes off the Griddle" by Billy Sunday; "Bobbed Hair, Bossy Wives, and Women Preachers" by John R. Rice; "The Devil Desires to Damn You" by Oliver B. Greene; "When God Hanged a Hippy" by Lester Roloff; "Get on the Water Wagon" by Billy Sunday; "Pitched His Tent Toward Sodom" by Bob Jones, Sr.; "God's Blockades on the Road to Hell" by R. A. Torrey.

One that I heard just recently that thrilled my heart was, "The Girl Who Wouldn't Wear Enough Clothes" by Maze Jackson. Other great sermons are: "The Believer's Three-Fold Judgment" by Curtis Hutson; "The Fool's Last Night on Earth" by T. DeWitt Talmadge; "Sin Is a Losing Game" by Tom Malone, Sr.; "But After This the Judgment" by B. R. Lakin; "God's Detective" by Billy Sunday; "The Great White Throne Judgment" by Jack Hyles; "Standing Idle amidst the Spoiling Harvest" by Tom Malone, Sr.; "Sinners in the Hands of an Angry God" by Jonathan Edwards; "When Skeletons Come Out of Their Closet" by John R. Rice; "The Devil's Boomerang" by Billy Sunday; "Don't Count Your Chickens before They Hatch" by Tom Malone, Sr.; "God's Three Deadlines" by J. Harold Smith; and "Payday Someday" by R. G. Lee.

Each preacher now in Heaven, preached every one of those sermons like Heaven was touching his head, Hell was boiling at his feet, and the Devil was within choking distance of him. Hey, Man of God, we should try that this coming Sunday morning. We should just go ahead and open a can of crazy. We should go ahead and kick the slats out of the thing. We should just go ahead, and PREACH!

Dr. Smith and I were recently in a conference where a mutual friend of ours had picked up another preacher on his way to the conference to sing. He told me that the preacher he picked up was somewhat discouraged. During that Sword Conference, he listened to Dr. Smith and me preach, and he said that God did something in his heart. He went back to his church, crawled into his pulpit, and preached like Billy Sunday back from the grave. They had people saved and families join the church. I got a message from my friend who said, "You'll never know the inspiration and influence that you had upon that preacher. He got back to his pulpit, and he just went ahead and preached." Friend, we ought to absolutely be broken, have a tear, and have a burden for our country when the pulpit has lost its trumpet.

I was in Street, Maryland, outside of Baltimore on my twenty-eighth anniversary of being saved. I go there every year during that week to preach for Dr. Randy Williams, Sr. On the actual night of my anniversary, I got back to the motel late. There were a number of text messages and voice mail messages from folks congratulating me on that anniversary. As I was working my way through the text messages and voice mail messages, I came to a message from Brother Benjamin Burkes who is the international director for Reformers Unanimous. Brother Burkes left this voice mail message, which said, "Doc, I'm preaching in Panama City, Florida, this weekend." (It was early Sunday morning that he left this message.) He said, "I heard you preach in that tent meeting in Rochester Hills, Michigan. You preached the sermon, 'What the Prodigal Found When He Finally Turned His Feet toward Papa's Farm'. I bought the CD from your book table, and God put it upon my heart to preach it this weekend."

He continued, "I went to McDonalds to find kind of a sequestered spot. I got my Bible, a legal pad, and a pen. I got the CD player and the CD, but had forgotten some earphones." Then he said, "I was going to preach your sermon, so I was listening to you preach, 'What the Prodigal Found When He Finally Turned His Feet toward Papa's Farm.'" And he added, "By the way, I need to tell you that this weekend in Panama City, Florida, there is a Harley Davidson Motorcycle Rally that's going on."

He continued, "I was listening to you preach, and across the McDonalds came a great big, burly, motorcycle enthusiast." Those were his words, "motorcycle enthusiast." If one were to take the Strong's Concordance and look up "motorcycle enthusiast" he would find "Biker Dude."

He said, "I was listening to you preach, 'What the Prodigal Found When He Finally Turned His Feet toward Papa's Farm,' and, across the McDonald's, this great big motorcycle enthusiast hollered, 'What is all that screaming?'"

Brother Benjamin Burkes said he hollered back, "That's preaching!"

Then the big, burly, motorcycle enthusiast said, "Who is it?"

Burkes said, "I yelled, 'It's Hamblin!'

The great big, burly, motorcycle enthusiast said, "Can I come over there and listen to that with you?"

Brother Burkes said, "Absolutely!"

The big, burly, motorcycle enthusiast got up and walked across that McDonalds and sat down. Brother Benjamin Burkes said, "After that fifty-five minute message, I looked at him, and tears were streaming down his cheeks. He said, 'I'm a prodigal. I left home when I was a teenager. I broke my mother's heart and my father's heart. They are both saved; they are now in Heaven.' He said, 'Not only do I need to get saved, but I want to get saved!'"

Brother Burkes said, "Right there in the shadow of the golden arches, John Stephens, 47 years of age, was birthed into the family of God!"

I believe it works. It works, Hallelujah, it works! What we ought to do in our churches is just turn everything else down, turn preaching up, and knock off the knob.

II. The Pew That Has Lost Its Testimony

Acts 5:1-2, *But a certain man named Ananias, with Sapphira his wife, sold a possession, And kept back part of the price, his wife also being*

"Give Me That Old-Time Religion!"

privy to it, and brought a certain part, and laid it at the apostles' feet. A distinct place that the believer should cry over because of the disastrous shape that it is in is the pew that has lost its testimony. In Acts 5: 1-2, the physician Luke, tells us that there was a married couple who set out to make people believe that they were more generous and greater Christians than anyone else in the early church. They sold a piece of property, kept back some of the hard cash, but wrote on their offering envelope in bold, big red ink, "We have given every penny from the sale of our parcel of pasture." One Bible student penned of them, "Their sin was in professing to give all while only giving some." They lied, and they lost their testimony. They also died. They joined the invisible choir early. By the way, if there is anyone who thinks that this sin stopped in the book of Acts, that this sin stopped in the early church, that this sin stopped at their premature graves, then see me because I have Elvis Presley's rookie baseball card that I will sell for a reasonable price. I wish it had stopped with them, but it continues to this day. We ought to have a burden, a tear, and an absolute brokenness when we see that the pew, especially the one that we often sit in, has lost its testimony.

There are several interesting things that happen when a believer loses his confirmation. Confirmation is that which gives one's words weight. First of all, he or she is deceitful with his or her purse. Acts 5:2, *And kept back part of the price...* A thing that transpires when a believer loses his confirmation, that which gives one's words weight, is that he is deceitful with his purse. What a child of God's checkbook reads says more about his walk with God than his favorite hymn that he requested to be sung in the next church service. How about, instead of telling our favorite hymn, we allow someone to look at our checkbook? How about, instead of saying what our favorite quartet is, we allow others to look at our expenditures from this month? That says more about our love for God than any other thing. When a believer loses his confirmation, that which gives one's words weight, he is deceitful with his purse.

A second thing that transpires when a believer loses his confirmation, that which gives one's words weight, is he is dishonorable with his partner. Acts 5:2 says, *...his wife also being privy to it....* When we lead a double life, we wickedly take our mate by the hand and lead him or her down the path of living a double life as well. That is a big statement, but I am not one bit hesitant or reticent to announce Mrs. Hamblin's cell phone number right now and have anyone call her, any day, any hour, any night, and just pose the question, "Is Dr. Hamblin a hypocrite? Is Dr. Hamblin one thing in a meeting and another thing out of the meeting? Is he one thing at home and another thing when he's not at home?" I am not one bit hesitant or reticent to do that.

It is my goal, if Jesus stays His coming, and I go before Mrs. Hamblin, that at my funeral, she will be able to say, "He was the greatest Christian I ever knew." We would have a revival that would make the headlines in the history books in Heaven if husbands and wives just got right with God. When we lose our confirmation, that which gives our words weight, we are then dishonorable with our partner.

A third thing that transpires when believers lose their confirmation, that which gives their words weight, is that they are disingenuous with their preacher. Acts 5:2, *...and brought a certain part, and laid it at the apostles' feet.* If what they said at the church door was true, then why is it that they are still living like Beelzebub's mother-in-law? That is wicked right there.

Imagine this for just a moment. See Ananias and Sapphira at the end of the service as they are walking out. Brother Peter is standing at the door of the temple and hears Brother Ananias say, "Oh, Brother Peter, I've never heard you any better."

Sister Sapphira says, "Oh, Brother Peter, that was a wonderful sermon on stewardship this morning. It so blessed and benefited our souls," Hey, Pinocchio, your nose is growing! I have been at this now for 30 years, and whenever I am in a revival meeting, tent meeting, or a Bible conference, after the first service someone comes to me and says, "Oh, Dr. Hamblin, we haven't heard preaching like that in decades." After hearing me one time! When they start to put that on, "That's wonderful! That's awesome! It was such a blessing. Man, you're Billy Sunday, Gypsy Smith, and Tom Malone, Sr. all rolled up in one," I just want to puke! When they say stuff like that, I realize they are not coming back. And, guess what? They do not come back!

"Give Me That Old-Time Religion!"

See, when we lose our confirmation that which gives our words weight, we are dishonorable with our preacher. Oh, that every single believer would realize the seriousness of this issue. What transpires, what takes place when we lose our confirmation is that we are deceitful with our purse, dishonorable with our partner, and disingenuous with our preacher.

More than a century and a half ago, the highland brigade of the British army was obligated to march across the Egyptian desert by night to Tell-el-Kebir. It would have been quite easy to lose the route, but a young naval officer volunteered to lead by stellar observation. So the soldiers looked to the sailor, and the sailor looked to the stars. The journey was completed by dawn, and the brigade charged the enemy's trenches and took them. The naval officer fell in the battle; however, as he lay dying, he turned his face to the general who was visiting the wounded and asked, "Sir, I led them straight, didn't I? I led them straight, didn't I? Sir, I led them straight, didn't I?" Hey, Child of God, the minute that our walk matches our talk, we will lead our family, our friends, and our fellow workers straight again. It is easy to weep over the saloon, and we ought to do it. It is easy to weep over the abortion clinic, and we ought to do it. It is easy to weep over the house of ill repute, and we should do it. But, when was the last time we looked at our own pew? When was the last time we just lingered a while on our own personal testimony and realized that our walk does not match our talk and our talk does not match our walk either?

III. The Path That Has Lost Its Travelers

Jeremiah 6:16 says, *Thus saith the LORD, Stand ye in the ways, and see, and ask for the old paths, where is the good way, and walk therein, and ye shall find rest for your souls. But they said, We will not walk therein.* The distinct place the believer should cry over because of the disastrous shape that it is in is the path that has lost its travelers. In Jeremiah 6:16, the prophet Jeremiah tells us about the only route on which God wanted His children to run up and down. He intends for His own to step on this old path when they get saved and stay on it until they step upon streets paved with pure gold. Anyone who has ever gotten saved and anyone who will ever get saved are saved on the old path. That is the only way. The Bible says in Acts 4:12, *...for there is none other name under heaven given among men, whereby we must be saved.* When a person gets saved, he does not get saved on a super highway. He gets saved on the old path. If it was good enough to bring us into the family of God, then it ought to be good enough for us to stick with it.

Every person who has his eyes fall on this verse, Jeremiah 6:16, needs to understand that ancient lanes are red-hot Bible preaching. I am talking about preaching like a cheap lawnmower, red-hot Bible preaching. Someone may ask, "How do you preach like a cheap lawnmower?" Loud, smoking, and wide open! These ancient lanes include red-hot Bible preaching, personal and ecclesiastical separation, inspired and preserved King James Bible, church on Sunday night, choir members and special music that are spirited but not sensual, hymns for the church service, confrontational soulwinning, revival meetings, weekly prayer meetings, *Sword of the Lord* conferences, camp meetings, lively worship, pastor-led congregations, modesty for all believers, and standards for workers. These are the ancient lanes.

Now, this is not a spiritual smorgasbord. One cannot say, "Well, I'll take a little bit of the King James Bible, but hymns for church..." The reason they are called hymns, is that they are about Him! God deliver us from this "seven-eleven" church music. Seven-eleven? Absolutely! It has about seven words, and people sing it eleven times. God deliver us from songs that do not even have the scriptural and spiritual depth of a rain puddle. Nothing beats "Amazing grace! how sweet the sound, that saved a wretch like me! I once was lost, but now am found, was blind, but now I see." Nothing is better than my favorite, "Jesus paid it all, all to Him I owe; sin had left a crimson stain, He washed it white as snow." Nothing beats, "At the cross, at the cross where I first saw the light, and the burden of my heart rolled away, it was there by faith I received my sight, and now I am happy all the day!" No other songs can beat the hymns in the hymnal. For every "old path" church that is in this country, there are ten "super highway" churches. And I ask the question, "Where are the Jeremiah Christians?" I ask the question, "Where are the Jeremiah children of God?" I ask the question, "Where are the Jeremiah believers who have a burden, who have a tear, who have a brokenness, when, in our country, the path has lost its travelers?"

The Bible says in II Timothy 3:14, *But continue thou in the things which thou hast learned and hast been assured of, knowing of whom thou hast learned them.* The reason there are bad Bibles, contemporary churches, and "ends-justifies-the-means" mindsets in ministries is that somebody did not continue in the things that they learned at the feet of some true, solid, and firm fundamentalist. I appreciate the fact that I never need to worry about the *Sword of the Lord.* I appreciate the fact that I never have to pick up a copy and wonder if there is liberal puke on the cover. By the way, those two words *liberal* and *puke* were birthed in the English language to be married. *Liberal* and *puke* go together like peanut butter and jelly. Dr. Smith and I serve on the cooperating board of the *Sword of the Lord.* It is a blessing that we are never embarrassed. It is a blessing that we never have to worry about picking up a copy and seeing somebody on there who should not even have the letters of his name sprinkled throughout an issue. It is a blessing to be able to get a publication that is not compromising, that is not capitulating, that is not throwing its arms around people who we should not throw our arms around. Thank God for a paper that knows what the old paths are and is determined and dedicated to stay there.

In recent days, people are losing their minds. It just absolutely staggers me. I do not know if they are sniffing glue or what, but people are just losing their minds, running with wrong crowds, and yoking up with people with whom they ought not to be. It absolutely blows my mind. Let us determine that we are not going to get off the old paths; we are not going to get off the ancient lanes; we are not bigger than the old paths; we are not bigger than the ancient lanes. Somebody ought to have a burden, a tear, and a brokenness when the path loses its travelers.

Dr. Bob Jones, Sr. once said, "There's a cure for backsliding, but there's no cure for apostasy." A few years ago, I was preaching in a meeting when a dear lady came to me after the service. She came to the book table, and said, "Dr. Hamblin, I heard you preach twenty-five years ago. In fact, in my purse is one of your preaching tapes that I bought twenty-five years ago. I've listened to it so many times that I can hardly

Does Any Christian Have a Tear?

even listen to it, and if I do listen to it, I have to turn it way up and put my ear to the tape recorder just to catch a word here and there."

She had not seen or heard me for twenty-five years. I said, "Ma'am, I've got to ask you a question. Please don't think that I'm looking for any kind of answer, but I've got to ask you the question. Whatever the answer is, I will accept it. Ma'am, is there any change? You've not heard me in twenty-five years. Is there any difference that you can see?"

She said, "I think you're more intense. I think you're more in-your-face, a little more smash-mouth, and a little bit more dogmatic. I think you're a little more dogmatic than you were back then, but it's the same thing."

Friend, every day there are preachers and people who are getting off the ancient lanes. We should not take our good pastor for granted. We should not take our church for granted because there is not a church like it on every corner; there is not a preacher like this in every pulpit. It seems like we absolutely are losing our minds and getting off the old paths. Somebody ought to be broken because of it.

One day, during the colonial times, a dark day occurred. In fact, it was May 19, 1780, in Hartford, Connecticut, when the sun seemed to disappear at mid-day. The people were so alarmed that many of them began to cry thinking the world was coming to an end. Even the legislature was disturbed and confused. Some wanted to adjourn without delay. One stalwart member, a Colonel Davenport said, "I make a motion that we secure some candles and proceed with our business. If the end of the world is about to come, I want to be found doing my duty."

Tune in Christian! I do not know if this is the end of the church age or not. But, I do know that there is a blanket of darkness, and I do know that there is a covering of depravity that blankets not only the world, but also our country. Whether these are the last days of the church age or not, I do not know, but I do know that darkness is upon us. So, I would make a suggestion. I would make a motion that we secure some candles; we light those candles; and we hold them high. I suggest that we stay on the old paths so that we might be found by God doing our duty. In Jeremiah 9:1, Jeremiah says, *Oh that my head*

"Give Me That Old-Time Religion!"

were waters, and mine eyes a fountain of tears... We have preached it. We have preached that we ought to weep over this, that, and the other thing in our country; and yes, we should. How about weeping for what goes on in the four walls of our churches, and how about weeping for what really goes on in the four fleshly walls of our hearts? The pulpit has lost its trumpet, the pew has lost its testimony, and the path has lost its travelers.

Chapter Three

Does the Devil Know You?

Acts 19:13-20 says, *Then certain of the vagabond Jews, exorcists, took upon them to call over them which had evil spirits the name of the Lord Jesus, saying, We adjure you by Jesus by whom Paul preacheth. And there were seven sons of one Sceva, a Jew, and chief of the priests, which did so. And the evil spirit answered and said, Jesus I know, and Paul I know; but who are ye? And the man in whom the evil spirit was leaped on them, and overcame them, and prevailed against them, so that they fled out of that house naked and wounded. And this was known to all the Jews and Greeks also dwelling at Ephesus; and fear fell on them all, and the name of the Lord Jesus was magnified. And many that believed came, and confessed, and shewed their deeds. Many of them also which used curious arts brought their books together, and burned them before all men: and they counted the price of them, and found it fifty thousand pieces of silver. So mightily grew the word of God and prevailed.*

I cannot read verse 19 without making some kind of comment. This is the crowd who uses Ouija boards. This is the crowd who uses tarot cards. This is the crowd who tells us to call them; and if we will give them our credit card number and its expiration date, they will tell us our future. If they could tell us our future, they could tell us what our credit card number was and its expiration date.

"Give Me That Old-Time Religion!"

The verse I would like to emphasis is verse 15: *And the evil spirit answered and said, Jesus I know, and Paul I know; but who are ye?* Does the Devil know you? There are few believers who, during their spiritual trek ever appear on Beelzebub's spiritual radar screen. Although we can find them faithfully sitting in a fundamental church, we cannot figure where Hell has felt any degree of their spiritual force. It is genuine salvation that makes one known in Heaven. It is Godly service that makes one known in Hell. Does the Devil know us? In Acts Chapter 19, we find the miracles of the Apostle Paul. This chapter can be easily outlined or laid out like this:

Verses 1-7 - The Revelation to the Converts
Verses 8-12 - The Revival throughout the Country
Verses 13-20 - The Reason for the Conflagration (just another word for big explosion with lots of fire)
Verses 21-34 - The Riot in the City
Verses 35-41 - The Remarks of the Clerk

It is while the physician Luke deals under the direct inspiration of the Holy Spirit with the reason for the conflagration, that we read the heart-wrenching question in verse 15, *And the evil spirit answered and said, Jesus I know, and Paul I know; but who are ye?* The word *know* in the Greek language means "to allow" or "to be aware." One well-known Bible student once wrote this about our text: "It was significant that within the realm of evil, demons knew both Christ and Paul and feared both." There could be no greater acknowledgement of the value of Paul's life and work. Never forget, that the more a leader accomplishes for God, the more aware the Prince of Darkness becomes of that same believer's activities and accomplishments. Do not miss this. It even bears repeating. The more a believer accomplishes for God, the more aware the Prince of Darkness becomes of that same believer's activities and accomplishments.

Friend, those of us who are saved should make sure that our efforts for Heaven are so effective that scores of them are felt in the deepest expanses of Hell. In Acts 19:15, the Son of God was known by

Does the Devil Know You?

the Devil, and a servant of God was known by the Devil as well. That ought to be our desire, our drive, and our spiritual destination. Just as Paul was known by the Devil, we should be known by the Devil as well. There are three outstanding things from the Apostle Paul's life that made him known by the Devil.

I. Powerful Praying

Acts 9:11, *And the Lord said unto him, Arise, and go into the street which is called Straight, and enquire in the house of Judas for one called Saul, of Tarsus: for, behold, he prayeth.* An outstanding thing that made the Apostle Paul known by the Devil was his powerful praying. In Acts 9:11, the physician Luke tells us that the place and posture that the seasoned Ananias would find the new convert Saul was on his knees. By finding him on his knees, the spiritual pattern would thereby be set for his spiritual life. There are just two small words, *he prayeth*. From his knees, this new convert will become an old disciple. Because of those two words, *he prayeth*, this will be the foundation, the jubilation, and the continuation of his spiritual life. From his knees, he will seize Heaven. From his knees, he will shake earth and scare Hell. The poet, W.T. Tooley must have had this apostle on his mind as he picked up his pen and put upon paper this soul-penetrating Poem, *Somebody Prayed*.

> A wandering sheep returned to the fold
> From whence it had long gone astray,
> What brought it back to the ninety and nine,
> The answer, somebody prayed.
>
> An Atheist heart, the sin-cleansing blood,
> Was applied in a marvelous way.
> He believed in the Christ Who died on the cross.
> God saved him when somebody prayed.
>
> On the bed of affliction, for years, one had laid.
> Death's dreaded sword over him swayed.
> But he rose from his bed, was restored to his strength,

God healed him when somebody prayed.

A Christian, whose labors and efforts seem vain,
Downhearted, discouraged, and dismayed,
Took up new courage and started again.
God answered when somebody prayed.

The harvest is ready, the laborers few.
Let's work while yet it is day,
For soon comes the night, when no man can work,
So while it's light, let us pray.

Friend, we will be known by the Devil and demons when we have powerful praying in our lives. The Bible says in Jeremiah 33:3, *Call unto me, and I will answer thee, and shew thee great and mighty things, which thou knowest not.* Where are the Christians whose prayer closets are the most despised places of the Devil on this earth? Where are the children of God who, when they fall to their knees, cause the Prince of Darkness to dial 911? Where are the believers whose prayer lists demand Beelzebub to double up on his heart medication when they are pulled out, lest he go into cardiac arrest?

A number of years ago, a dear preacher friend of mine in Talbott, Tennessee, gave me a small booklet on the prayer life of Daniel Nash. I would recommend it to anyone. Daniel Nash was a preacher who traveled with Charles Finney. He did not share a great pulpit ministry, but a great prayer ministry with Finney. Four months after Daniel Nash died, Finney left his itinerate ministry for a pastorate. He went four more months in meetings, and then, seemingly for no reason at all, left his schedule and evangelism and went into the pastorate. Maybe this is the reason. Often Nash would go before Finney, secure a room, and do nothing but pray up until and even through the meeting. One time he rented a dark, damp cellar for twenty-five cents a week for the period of the Finney meeting which lasted two long weeks. He and another man in that cell battled the forces of darkness. Is it any wonder that when Daniel Nash died, Finney decided that maybe it was time to leave evangelism? I read in that small, heart-challenging booklet that Daniel Nash's grave is in upstate New York. It is in an old, abandoned cemetery at a church where he once pastored. There is a small stone that marks the spot and it reads: *Daniel Nash: Pastor, 1816-1822; Laborer with Finney, Mighty in Prayer; Nov 27, 1775-Dec 20, 1831.* Christian, it is those few-and-far-between believers who are mighty in prayer who are known in the charred caverns of Hell! How does the Devil know us? The Devil should know us by our powerful praying!

II. Plain Preaching

Acts 19:8 says, *And he went into the synagogue, and spake boldly for the space of three months, disputing and persuading the things concerning the kingdom of God.* An outstanding thing in the Apostle Paul's life that made him known by the Devil was his plain preaching. In Acts 19:8, the physician Luke tells us that when the Apostle Paul entered Ephesus, he immediately gave his energies to edifying the people and to evangelistic preaching. I think one must pay very close attention to the key words in this verse. The key words are *synagogue, spake boldly,* and *three months*. That means that the Moses of the New Testament walked into a religious den of the Devil, pulled both hammers back on his Gospel gun, and, for ninety-two days, blew the hair, hide, and head off anything that even thought about moving. Friend, we should be known by the Devil because of our plain preaching.

I like singing, and I am married to a wonderful, Godly, anointed musician. But I think in our fundamental, independent, Bible-believing, Bible-preaching, pre-millennial, missionary-minded, soulwinning, temperamental Baptist churches, we need to dial down the music and dial up the preaching. There is not an ill in this nation, there is not a sin in this country, there is not a problem in our land that could not be cured, challenged, and corrected if men of God just stood up with the Word of God and, led by the Spirit of God, absolutely "let it rip!" We need to get back to preaching in our churches, not story telling. I tell stories. I told one just a moment ago, and it moved my heart. I am not preaching against telling stories, but there is nothing like Bible preaching. Our

"Give Me That Old-Time Religion!"

nation is starving for men of God who will just get up, open the Bible, and preach the Bible.

I was at a meeting recently where they had one hour and forty-nine minutes of singing. I timed it. One hour and forty-nine minutes of singing absolutely wore out the crowd. Then they turned it over to me as if I were some kind of miracle worker. Both they and I were worn out. Pardon me, but after all that singing, I wanted to go to the movies. Just song after song after song! I like raspberry pie, but after seventeen slices, one will not even know it is raspberry pie. They wore out the crowd, and they wore me out. I am not like you visitors from Heaven. I get in the flesh. Singing that long wore me out. They finally turned the pulpit over to me. I checked my calendar to see if the date had changed since the service started. I made some kind of introductory remarks. I said, "I have a philosophy. For every minute of singing, there will be an hour and a half of preaching. According to my watch, we sang for one hour and forty-nine minutes." God did not say that singing would save the world. God did not say that singing is the answer. God said that preaching is the answer. We need to get back to just plain preaching!

Children need preaching. Teenagers need preaching. Adults need preaching. Senior citizens need preaching. Everybody needs preaching. Everybody in the church can be benefited and blessed by preaching. Let us turn down everything else and turn up the preaching. There are three subjects that the apostle Paul was straightforward about in his sermons.

First of all, Paul was straightforward on the deity of the Saviour. Acts 9:20 says, *And straightway he preached Christ in the synagogues, that he is the Son of God.* It is interesting that this was the very first sermon that Paul preached. His first sermon dealt with the deity of the Lord Jesus Christ.

Two weeks ago, I was preaching in Oakland, Maryland. The motel where I was staying would give you a complimentary copy of the *USA Today*. There was a huge article on the front page about the Gospel according to Judas. The reporter went on and on and wasted much paper and ink expounding on all the values of the Gospel according to Judas. That is not in my Bible. Judas did not write a Gospel. In fact, if

Judas wrote anything, it was a postcard from Hell that said, "It sure is hot down here." Jesus is the Son of God. He and Judas were not buddies. They did not switch places. Judas did not go to the Cross. Jesus did not sneak out. One would have to be stupid on several different levels to believe that.

Secondly, he was straightforward on the topic of the deception of the sinner. Acts 17:22, *Then Paul stood in the midst of Mars' hill, and said, Ye men of Athens, I perceive that in all things ye are too superstitious.* When a preacher lowers the blade on prayer cloths, bottles of healing water, rosary beads, incense, confessing one's sins to a "so-called" father, giving up bubble gum for lent, holy underwear, being baptized from the dead, trying to pedal a ten-speed into Heaven, not receiving blood transfusions, or never saluting the American flag – when a preacher lowers the blade on that stuff, I believe that the Apostle Paul, in Heaven, shouts, "Amen!"

Thirdly, the Apostle Paul was straightforward on the topic of the design of the saint. Acts 22:10 says, *And I said, What shall I do, Lord?* The reason we have scores of church members who think that the pinnacle of the Christian life is just to sit on a church pew on Sunday mornings is that no preacher has told them otherwise. The pinnacle of the Christian life is not taking up pew space. The pinnacle of being a Bible college student is not getting a girlfriend. Oh, that every single person would realize that the subjects that the Apostle Paul straightforwardly dealt with in his preaching were the deity of the Saviour, the deception of the sinner, and the design of the saint. It is that type of preaching that makes the Devil cuss so badly that there is no soap factory in the world that can produce enough cleansing agent to wash out his mouth.

Back in the early nineteenth century, there was a fearless preacher whose name was Peter Cartwright. Peter Cartwright was an old-fashioned, circuit-riding minister. One Sunday, he was preaching in a very large, dignified church. During the song service, just before he was to take the pulpit, the pastor leaned over and whispered to him that General Andrew Jackson had just entered the building. He cautioned Cartwright to be very careful in what he said, lest he offend their famous guest. Brother Cartwright was determined not to compromise the truth.

"Give Me That Old-Time Religion!"

He knew that great leaders needed the Lord just as much as anyone else. When he was about halfway through his message, he stopped and looked around. Then he said, "I understand that General Andrew Jackson is in the crowd this morning. I want General Jackson to know that, if he doesn't get saved, he will die and go to Hell just like anybody else." I don't know, but I can imagine that the pastor passed out. Heart palpitations! When the service was over, Andrew Jackson sought out the preacher and received the Lord Jesus Christ as his personal Saviour.

He became a true and trusted friend of Peter Cartwright for the rest of their lives. We need to get back to plain preaching. There should be no strings in the pulpit, no shackles on the pulpit, and no controls on the pulpit other than those placed by the Spirit of God, the Word of God, and the God of Heaven. He is the only One Who ought to control the pulpit!

> **There should be no strings in the pulpit, no shackles on the pulpit, and no controls on the pulpit other than those placed by the Spirit of God, the Word of God, and the God of Heaven.**

III.   Persistent Personal Soulwinning

Acts 20:26 says, *Wherefore I take you to record this day, that I am pure from the blood of all men.* An outstanding characteristic of the Apostle Paul's life that made him known by the Devil was his persistent, personal soulwinning. In Acts 20:26, the physician Luke tells us that the Apostle Paul was saying at the close of his dissertation, the close to his deliberate discourse to the elders of Ephesus, how that he was steadfast in evangelism.

One may say, "Well, I don't see evangelism in that verse. I don't hear soulwinning in that verse. I don't see witnessing in that verse."

Listen again to what Paul states, *I am pure from the blood of all men.* We will never understand that phrase without referring back to the Old Testament. The Bible says in Ezekiel 3:18, *When I say unto the wicked, Thou shalt surely die; and thou givest him not warning, nor speakest to warn the wicked from his wicked way, to save his life; the same wicked man shall die in his iniquity; but his blood will I require at thine hand.* Paul was saying, "There is not one sinner in the entire city of Ephesus whose blood is on my hands. I have warned and witnessed to everyone."

We need that. We need that in our churches and in our colleges. Pardon me, college student. If one is not a soulwinner, what makes him think that a diploma will make him a soulwinner? If one does not come out on visitation, what makes him think he will come out on visitation when he gets a diploma? A diploma, a cap, a gown, and a tassel do not make a person a soulwinner. If he is not doing it now, he is not going to do it later. If one does not pass out Gospel tracts now, he will not pass out Gospel tracts when he graduates from a fundamental Bible college. If one does not carry a soulwinner's New Testament now, he is not going to carry one when he graduates. A soulwinner's New Testament is small enough for guys to stick in their pockets or girls to put in their purses. We need them when we sneak up on sinners. When we carry a family Bible, we are going to scare them. They are going to think that we are nuts. God is going to think we are nuts, too!

The Apostle Paul was the kind of Christian who was soulwinning from the time he picked his head up from his pillow to the time he put his head down that night. From the start of the day to the stop of the day, the Devil was always miserable because he knew that Paul would be continually working to bring people into the family of God.

Friend, we should be known by the Devil by our persistent, personal soulwinning. The Bible says in Luke 14:23, *And the lord said unto the servant, Go out into the highways and hedges, and compel them to come in, that my house may be filled.* By the way, if the house could not be filled, Jesus would not have sent us out. He told us that if we go, we will get things done. But we do not get things done unless we go. Where are the Christians who put Gospel tracts in their pockets at the beginning of a new day so that the Devil weeps? Where are the children of God who pick up their

> *Where are the Christians who put Gospel tracts in their pockets at the beginning of a new day so that the Devil weeps?*

"Give Me That Old-Time Religion!"

personal worker's New Testaments, causing Satan to start to swear? Where are the believers who show up for church-wide soulwinning, causing the Prince of Darkness to eat Tums and wash them down with Maalox? Where are they?

A preacher who was like the Apostle Paul in his soulwinning was Dwight Lyman Moody. Mr. Moody saw a little girl standing on the street with a pail in her hand. He went up to her and invited her to Sunday school. She promised to go the following Sunday, but she did not do so. Mr. Moody watched for her for weeks. Then one day, he saw her on the street again at some distance from him. He started toward her, but she saw him and started to run away. Mr. Moody followed her. She went down one street and Mr. Moody went after her. She went up another street and Mr. Moody followed her. She went through an alley with Mr. Moody still following. Down another street she went, and Mr. Moody was hot on her heels. Then she dashed into a saloon. That is probably where we would have stopped. No, we would not have stopped there because we would not have even started. She dashed into a saloon, and Mr. Moody dashed after her. She ran out the back door and up a flight of stairs. Mr. Moody was still following. She threw herself under the bed, and Mr. Moody reached under the bed and pulled her out by the foot and led her to Christ.

He found that her mother was a widow who once had seen better circumstances, but had gone down until she was living over a saloon. I think you are smart enough to know what all that entailed. She had several children. Mr. Moody led the mother and all of the family to Christ. When Dwight L. Moody pulled that little child out from under the bed by the foot, he was pulling a whole family into the Kingdom of God.

It sure would please me to be a soulwinner like that. If I could be a soulwinner like that, I know it would displease the Devil. Let us just go ahead and decide and determine that if Jesus was known by the Devil and He is the Son of God, and Paul was known by the Devil and he was a servant of God, that we, as servants of God, can be known by the Devil too. Does the Devil know you?

Chapter Four

Stay on Straight Street

Acts 9:10-16 says, *And there was a certain disciple at Damascus, named Ananias; and to him said the Lord in a vision, Ananias. And he said, Behold, I am here, Lord.* I cannot read verse 10 without making some kind of comment. Notice that Jesus knew the name of one of his servants. I am glad that it does not matter who the saint of God is or who the servant of God may be, Jesus is very mindful of that person's name. He does not need to wear a name tag. Jesus does not have to have a personal assistant who whispers into His ear the names of His children or the names of His servants. Jesus knows who we are if we are saved, and He knows who we are if we are His servants. In fact, in one of the Gospels, we read of the conversion of Zacchaeus. Jesus knows not only the names of His servants and His children, but also the names of those who are not His servants and not His children. Verse 11, *And the Lord said unto him, Arise, and go into the street which is called Straight and enquire in the house of Judas for one called Saul, of Tarsus: for, behold, he prayeth, And hath seen in a vision a man named Ananias coming in, and putting his hand on him, that he might receive his sight. Then Ananias answered, Lord, I have heard by many of this man, how much evil he hath done to thy saints at Jerusalem: And here he hath authority from the chief priests to bind all that call on thy name. But the Lord said unto him, Go*

"Give Me That Old-Time Religion!"

thy way: for he is a chosen vessel unto me, to bear my name before the Gentiles, and kings, and the children of Israel: For I will shew him how great things he must suffer for my name's sake. Look back at verse 11, *And the Lord said unto him, Arise, and go into the street which is called Straight, and enquire in the house of Judas for one called Saul, of Tarsus: for, behold, he prayeth.*

Today there is a temptation for the believer to move from the turnpike of truth to the expressway of error. The world, the flesh, and the Devil are doing their best to make their highways alluring. But God's richest blessings can only be found on His divine boulevard. Stay on Straight Street! In Acts 9:10-16 we find the concern of Ananias. This chapter can be easily outlined or laid out like this:

   Verses 1-9 - The Conversion of Saul
   Verses 10-16 - The Concern of Ananias
   Verses 17-22 - The Confession of Faith
   Verses 23-31 - The Confidence of Barnabas
   Verses 32-35 - The Command to Aeneas
   Verses 36-43 - The Challenge to Peter

It is while the physician Luke is dealing under the direct inspiration of the Holy Spirit with the concern of Ananias that a person reads about the new convert, Paul. He is starting his Christian life and staying in a home on Straight Street. The word *straight* in the Greek language means "to be level" or "to be true." I have read that this street is actually still in existence in Damascus. It gets its name because it is perfectly straight and level. It runs from east to west and, again, is extremely straight. It is very interesting to note that this word in the Greek language is the same word that is used before Acts 9:11 to describe the ministry of John the Baptist. This word *straight* is found not only in Acts 9:11, but also in Matthew 3:3. Before we ever get to our text, before we ever get to this section of Scripture, before we ever get to this part and portion of the Word of God, Acts 9:11, we see that in Mathew 3:3, the same Greek word is used in describing and detailing the ministry of John the Baptist. There the Bible says, *For this is he that was spoken of by the prophet Esaias, saying, The voice of one crying in the wilderness, Prepare ye the way of the Lord, make his paths straight.* The physical avenue on which Paul was found is the very same spiritual avenue on which believers should be found today. It could have been called Rocco Road, Scenic Circle Drive South, Kenmore, North Street, South Street, Brown Lane, or Oakwood Boulevard. Out of all the names that that street could have been called, it is interesting and intriguing that the name of the street was Straight. We ought to remain straight on some things. I realize we live in a day where crookedness, perverseness, and numerous changes are prevalent, but it is still my conviction and, yes, even my contention that there are some things on which the child of God and the Church of God must continue to remain firm, straight, and right. Let us look at some of these things.

I. The Scriptures

II Timothy 3:16 says, *All scripture is given by inspiration of God, and is profitable for doctrine, for reproof, for correction, for instruction in righteousness.* The believer should stay on Straight Street when it comes to the Scriptures. In II Timothy 3:16, the Apostle Paul tells us that all of the Bible has been divinely inspired by God. It is completely free from human error. Evangelist Oliver B. Greene, God bless his sainted memory, once said, "The sixty-six books in our Bible contain all that anyone needs to know about time, eternity, God, the Devil, Heaven, Hell, salvation, damnation, sin, and righteousness." He went on to say, "Anything we need to know about our relationship to God and His relationship to us is found in the Bible."

Today there are people who say, "The Bible is 90% accurate and 10% inaccurate. The Scriptures are inspired on a thought level and not a word level, and we need the newest translation to understand the Bible." Those who make such statements have deliberately departed from this important road. Friend, we must stay on Straight Street when it comes to the Scriptures. The Bible says in Psalm 119:89, *For ever, O Lord, thy word is settled in heaven.* Now, if the Bible is settled in Heaven, then the Bible ought to be settled on earth, in the heart of the child of God, and in the heart of the church of God. Bible honouring church

"Give Me That Old-Time Religion!"

members should be glad that their church is not a member of the "Bible of the Month" club. The people of that church should be glad that they will not have to hear the NIV, the RSV, the ASV, or the MICKEY MOUSE version from their pulpit. They are going to hear the Bible, the King James Bible, the inspired, inerrant, infallible, impeccable Word of God. There are seven wonders of the Word of God:

1. The Wonder of Its Formation - The way in which it grew is one of the mysteries of time.
2. The Wonder of Its Unification - It is a library of sixty-six books, yet one book.
3. The Wonder of Its Age - It is the most ancient of all books.
4. The Wonder of Its Sale - It is the bestseller of all time. More copies have been sold than any other book.
5. The Wonder of Its Interest - It is the only book in the world read by all classes of people.
6. The Wonder of Its Language - It was written largely by uneducated men, yet it is the best book from a literary standpoint.
7. The Wonder of Its Preservation - It is the most hated of all books, yet it continues to exist.

People say, "Dr. Hamblin, when you say things like that, you give the impression that you are King James only."

My reply is, "Congratulations! Yes, I am King James only. In fact, I am so King James only that I think you ought to spell it in capital letters." We do not belong to the "Bible of the Month" club. We are not waiting for some new version (I should say "perversion") or some new translation (I should say "trash-lation") to come out to understand the mind of God. If God were to give people passes to come back to their churches after they have gone to Heaven, they ought to be able to follow along in their same King James Bibles. They should not have to get a new version or translation to follow along.

I remember reading this story, and it blessed my heart. There was a Christian who was packing a suitcase for a long business trip.

He was putting the last few things in his suitcase. He said to a friend, "There's still a little corner in which I desire to pack a little guidebook, a lamp, a mirror, a telescope, a book of poems, a number of biographies, a bundle of old letters, a hymn book, a sharp sword, and a small library."

"How are you going to do that?" queried his friend.

In response, the Christian picked up his Bible and delicately placed it in that open corner. Christian, as we go on this spiritual sojourn, we had better make sure that we have a Bible. We had better make sure that we have the Word of God. We had better make sure that we have the Scriptures as we go on this spiritual sojourn, for we will never succeed and will always fail without a Bible!

II. Separation

Philippians 2:15 says, *That ye may be blameless and harmless, the sons of God, without rebuke, in the midst of a crooked and perverse nation, among whom ye shine as lights in the world.* The believer should stay on Straight Street when it comes to separation. In Philippians 2:15, the Apostle Paul tells us that saved people are to live a Godly life among the lost. When they do this, they will stand out all the more clearly against the dark background of this world. I can never think of Philippians 2:15 without thinking of the simple illustration of what kind of light we are. That verse tells us that we are lights in the world. We know that there are all kinds of different lights. There are flashlights, floodlights, and car headlights. This verse talks about how a Christian is a light in the world. We can be a penlight for Jesus, a nightlight for Jesus, or we can be one of those great big searchlights that they put in the parking lot of used car dealerships when they have a great big used car sale. I do not want to be a penlight. I do not even want to be a nightlight. I would like to be one of those great big lights for the Lord Jesus Christ. It is up to us to decide and determine how bright our light is going to be by determining how separated we live our Christian lives.

There are people who say, "We don't want to live in such a way that would cause others to think that we're narrow-minded. To reach the world, we must resemble the world, and as long as we're winning people to Christ, it really doesn't matter who we're running with." My

"Give Me That Old-Time Religion!"

response is, "Excuse me! When you make statements like that you have deliberately departed from this important lane." Friend, we must stay on Straight Street when it comes to separation!

There are three vital parts to Biblical separation. When I say Biblical separation, I am talking about separation that is in the Bible. There are many things that are called separation that are not really separation, but prejudice or preference. I am not talking about prejudice. I am not talking about preference.

I have some preferences and prejudices in my life. For instance, I have a prejudice on a candy. I like Milk Duds. I absolutely love Milk Duds. The only thing better than a box of Milk Duds is another box of Milk Duds. I absolutely love Milk Duds, and that is something that I have a prejudice toward. I am not saying that if people eat Paydays, York Peppermint Patties, or Reese's Peanut Butter Cups, they are going to Hell on a bullet train; but at the same time, my favorite candy in all the universe is Milk Duds. Now, if I went on a crusade and preached that people are not right with God if they do not love Milk Duds, there would be a little problem with that in that I would have no Bible to back me up. So, that is a preference and a prejudice because I have no Bible verse for it.

A conviction is something for which there is a chapter and verse. A conviction is something that is found in the Bible. I hear preachers preach against things that are absolutely nowhere in the Word of God. I have heard preachers preach against colored shirts. I have heard preachers preach against how many buttons a suit coat has. Every time an idiot preaches that, I run out and buy a suit with one more button. There were three sisters who used to sing with me. At the time when we were preaching and singing together, three-button suits had just come back in style. Those three sisters told me, "Our dad preached the other night that if you wear a three-button suit, you're a sissy."

I said, "Really?"

Those three sisters said, "Yeah, that's what Dad said."

I said, "That's interesting." I took that and filed it in the filing cabinet of my memory.

About six months later, their dad and I were together in a meeting, and he was wearing a three-button suit. When the service was over, and he and I were alone, I pulled him aside and said, "My Brother, is there something that you need to tell me? Are you coming out of the closet?"

He dropped his head as if he had been shot, and he said, "You know what, Doc, that was pretty stupid what I said."

I said, "Yes, sir. It was extremely stupid."

When I say separation, I am not talking about a prejudice or a preference; I am talking about something that is in the Bible.

The Biblical doctrine of separation basically deals with three different things. First of all, separation deals with attitude. Romans 12:2 says, *And be not conformed to this world: but be ye transformed by the renewing of your mind, that ye may prove what is that good, and acceptable, and perfect, will of God.* The Biblical doctrine of separation mentioned here deals with attitude. No believer will ever live a separated life until he first has a separated mind. If a person starts with just the hem and the haircut before he starts with the heart, he will be a Pharisee. If separation does not start in our hearts, and it begins with our hems and our haircuts, then that is not separation. We will end up being Pharisees. We will end up looking down at people and end up thinking we are "all that and a bag of flaming hot Cheetos." So it deals with attitudes.

> *No believer will ever live a separated life until he first has a separated mind.*

Secondly, the Biblical doctrine of separation deals with alliances or partnerships. II Corinthians 6:14 says, *Be ye not unequally yoked together with unbelievers...* The saint who is holding hands with the sinner for a spiritual cause is wrong. That is the reason that we do not yoke up with every donkey that brays a verse of Scripture. That is the reason why we are not Promise Keepers and we do not go to the Billy Graham Crusades. That is the reason that we do not run with this or that crowd and we are not backward about saying why. It is all because separation deals with alliances. Consider a saint who is wrongly holding hands with a sinner for a spiritual cause. When the sinner is seen doing

"Give Me That Old-Time Religion!"

wrong, a good saint who is holding hands with the straying saint is tainted also. There are many people who absolutely do not understand what separation is. When the preacher preaches on it, they think he is a killjoy. When the preacher preaches on it, they think he is being mean and cranky and must have gotten in a fight with his wife on the way to work. They just automatically assume he has a bee in his bonnet, he has his tail in a twist, or that something is wrong with him.

Let me try to illustrate. A good Christian and a bad Christian are yoked together. The bad Christian has a bad Bible and is a liberal puke. He goes to Rick Warren's saddleback conferences, stands one way one day and another way another day. Now, the good Christian has a King James Bible and is a rock-ribbed fundamentalist, but is a little weak on separation because he does not realize the importance of it. So this good Christian and this liberal puke are joined together. All of a sudden, I yoke up with this Christian brother who is joined with this liberal puke. I am then joined up with somebody with whom I should not be.

Dr. Malone used to say, "I'm not a bridge builder. I'm not interested in building bridges. In fact, I've got a pocketful of matches, willing to burn any bridge that yokes up to the wrong person now."

I know it seems almost out-of-step and antiquated, but I told a preacher today, "I'm old school. Call me a caveman or a dinosaur. I'm just old school."

There ought to be separation in the work of God. That is as simple as I can tell it. So, we need to pay attention when the pastor says, "We're not having the Gideons come. That truck is going down the road the wrong way. The Gideons put bad Bibles in motels and in soldier's hands." We do not want to support something like that, do we? The first thing we have to be straight on is the Scriptures. That is why we do not support the Gideons. That is why we do not send the bus to the Franklin Graham Festival. That is why we do not have *Daily Bread* laying around. We do not want any holding hands or yoking or running with somebody with whom we ought not to be running. I am so convinced that this is important.

Years ago at a meeting, there was a mall near the motel where I was staying. One afternoon, I went to the mall. They had a very nice

Stay on Straight Street

exclusive men's store in the mall, and I bought a sharp necktie from that store. I put it in my closet, and I said that I was going to wear it for a special occasion. I was home from a meeting one night, and Mrs. Hamblin and I were watching the *Old-Time Gospel Hour*. As we were watching the *Old-Time Gospel Hour*, Jerry Falwell came on, and he had on that necktie, the same one that I had bought. I said to Mrs. Hamblin, "I can't believe it." I wanted to wear that tie, but I am so convinced that separation is right, I have never worn that tie. I keep it. I look at it and get as mad as the Devil because it is an awesome tie, but I do not want to wear a tie that a compromiser wore. I do not want to wear a tie that a liberal wore. I do not want to wear the same tie that somebody who does not have a Bible and who does not have a firm stand and does not know fundamentalism wore. I do not want to wear the tie he wore. Separation has to do with whom we have alliances.

Separation has to do with attire. The Biblical doctrine of separation deals not only with attitude and alliances or partnerships but also with attire. I Timothy 2:9 says, *In like manner also, that women* [and I guess we could inject right here, and men] *adorn themselves in modest apparel...* A vital part of the Biblical doctrine of separation is attire. The Christian should not care if the tag on his clothes reads Calvin Klein, just as long as it reads Modest Apparel. Lately, I have been preaching that a Christian ought to have just "church clothes." I do not know what "non-church clothes" are. I can wear all of my clothes to church. If one cannot wear "non-church clothes" to church, one ought not to wear them in the world! Let us go a little bit further. If one would not wear his church clothes to the beach, then why in God's name would he wear his beach clothes to the church? It is amazing. Beach clothes are less than underwear, and it is amazing that if it is florescent, polka dotted, or striped, then it is all right! I do not care what it has on it. If someone would not wear his church clothes to the beach, then why in God's name would he wear his beach clothes to the church! A Christian ought to just look like a Christian!

I could not tell the times that I have flown in the middle of the night. I fly just the way I look when I am preaching. That is how I fly. I could not tell the number of times flight attendants have come to me and said, "Preacher, can I ask you a Bible question?" "Preacher, can I give you a prayer request?" "Preacher, can I ask about current events?"

I do not have a button that says "preacher" on me. In the middle of the night, on an airplane some thirty plus thousand feet in the air, people will come to me and say, "What do you think about this verse?" "Can I give you a prayer request?" "Can I ask you a question?" People would not tolerate it for one second if I showed up in a pair of shorts, nor should they. People would be upset, and rightfully so. If separation is good for a preacher, it is good for a church member, too. If separation is good for a preacher, it is good for Christians, too.

We have almost lost our minds when it comes to separation. If we get any more casual than what we are in the house of God, I believe people are going to be showing up in bathrobes and pajamas and great big fuzzy slippers!

Separation has to do with attire. Now, that is not just women dressing right. That is men dressing right, too. In my thirty-one years of being in the ministry and crisscrossing this nation, I have seen more men than women dress immodestly in the house of God. I have seen men who ought to know better than to show up at church with their shirt unbuttoned all the way down to their belly button. If women ought to dress right, men ought to dress right too. It was a happy day when my mother let me wear long pants. I see men wearing shorts. It is absolutely hilarious. Saved men are wearing shorts. Grown men are wearing shorts. I want to say to them, "Can I help you cross the street, little boy?" Do we still believe in separation? The Biblical doctrine of separation deals with attitude, alliances, and attire. We must stay straight on it.

Do not think the preacher is a crank or a grouch or unreasonable when he says, "You know what, we're saved, we ought to look like we're saved." When the maniac of Gadarenes got saved, he did not take off more clothes, he put on more clothes. When we are walking with God, we should not be shedding clothes; we should be trying to put on more clothes. Oh, that every person would realize that the vital parts of Biblical separation are attitude and alliances and attire.

When Gypsy Smith's father heard the message of salvation with penance, he received the Saviour as his own. That evening Gypsy

Smith's father returned to his motherless children in the Gypsy wagon and related to them all that he knew of the Saviour and the Scriptures. Then he prayed with them, setting up a family altar on the first night of his new life in Christ. The following morning, he repeated the whole matter again. Then he went back to town and took with him the dearest treasure of a Gypsy's heart, his violin. Upon returning home that night, he was without it for he had sold it. He had sufficient spiritual insight that first day of salvation to realize that the old association with drinking and dancing places where he used his violin was inconsistent with his stand for Christ. It tormented his own conscience.

Christian, may I say that we ought to get rid of the "violin," whatever it may be that is wrecking and ruining our walk with God. We have to remain straight when it comes to separation. Genesis 1:1-4 says, *In the beginning God created the heaven and the earth. And the earth was without form, and void; and darkness was upon the face of the deep. And the Spirit of God moved upon the face of the waters. And God said, Let there be light: and there was light. And God saw the light, that it was good: and God divided the light from the darkness.* We are not even five verses deep in the first book of the Bible, and God is talking about separation. God is saying, "We've got light over here." And, God is saying, "We've got dark over here." God Himself divided them because God believes in separation.

III. Simple Plan of Salvation

Romans 10:9 says, *That if thou shalt confess with thy mouth the Lord Jesus, and shalt believe in thine heart that God hath raised him from the dead, thou shalt be saved.* The believer should stay on Straight Street when it comes to the simple plan of salvation. In Romans 10:9, the Apostle Paul tells us that lost people can be saved by simply accepting the truth of the Gospel and by receiving the Lord Jesus Christ as their personal Saviour. It is totally of God and not of man. Charles Haddon Spurgeon once said, "One might better try to sail the Atlantic in a paper boat than to get to Heaven in good works." Today there are people who say a person cannot be saved after hearing the Gospel only one time. They say that unless a person changes his ways, God will not save

"Give Me That Old-Time Religion!"

him and that he really did not get saved if he has ever sinned since his profession of faith. Those who make such statements have deliberately departed from this important avenue.

Friend, we should stay on Straight Street when it comes to the simple plan of salvation. The Bible says in John 3:16, *For God so loved the world, that he gave his only begotten Son, that whosoever believeth in him should not perish, but have everlasting life.* If God made it easy for us to be saved, why do we want to turn around and make it hard for other people to be saved? If it were hard, we would not have been saved; but because it is simple, children can be saved, adults can be saved, and teenagers and senior citizens can be saved too. It is a simple plan of salvation. It is not rocket science. One does not need to be a Nobel Peace Prize winner or have multiple degrees behind his name. All a person has to do is realize that he is a sinner and God is a big Saviour, and if he will come to Him, He will save him for time and eternity. Salvation is simple. I am glad it is easy. I am glad anybody can get saved. We must remain straight on salvation.

Some people may say, "Well, I don't think that everybody who professes to be saved really is saved." I agree, "Yes, some may be lost; but the fact still remains that anybody can get saved because it is a simple plan of salvation." We should be glad that it is easy. We should be glad that it is simple. We should be glad that when we got saved, we did not need to take a test, matriculate from some school of higher learning, do a correspondence course, or prepare and study to take five tests and fail four of them to get saved. We just simply said, "Yes" to Jesus. Jesus moved in, and we were saved.

There once was a poor woman who greatly desired a bunch of grapes from the king's conservatory for her sick child who was near death. She took half a crown and went to the king's gardener to try to purchase the grapes, but was rudely repulsed. A second effort with more money met like results. It happened that the king's daughter heard the angry words of the gardener and the crying of the woman and inquired into the matter. When the poor woman had told her story, the princess said, "My dear woman, you are mistaken. My father is not a merchant, but a king. His business is not to sell, but to give." Whereupon she plucked the bunch from the vine and gently dropped them into the woman's apron. Hallelujah! My Saviour is not a merchant, but a King, and He does not sell salvation. He does not give indulgences for salvation. He does not give salvation if someone lights a candle, counts some beads, goes swimming in the baptistry, or kisses the Pope's toe. People do not understand that a person cannot earn salvation. He must simply receive it. We must remain on Straight Street when it comes to the simple plan of salvation.

In Acts Chapter 9, Saul of Tarsus gets saved. He will later be known as the Apostle Paul. Ananias is told by God, "I want you to make a follow-up call." Follow-up is in the Bible. Soulwinning is not about getting a notch on one's New Testament.

I like what one preacher said about follow-up. "We're to win them, we're to work them, and we're to wet them." God sends Ananias to make this follow-up call, and He said that Ananias would find Saul on Straight Street. That is where we ought to be found. That is where we ought to be helping our pastor.

Churches are losing their minds. Churches are going contemporary. Churches are absolutely going crazy. There are churches that are throwing out the Bible, throwing out the hymnbook, throwing out Sunday night services, and throwing out Wednesday night prayer meetings. Churches are no longer separated. That should mean, all the more, that we need to stand firm in what we believe. Stay on Straight Street.

"Give Me That Old-Time Religion!"

Chapter Five

My Three Fears as a Fundamentalist

I Corinthians 9:19-24 says, *For though I be free from all men, yet have I made myself servant unto all, that I might gain the more. And unto the Jews I became as a Jew, that I might gain the Jews; to them that are under the law, as under the law, that I might gain them that are under the law; To them that are without law, as without law, (being not without law to God, but under the law to Christ,) that I might gain them that are without law. To the weak became I as weak, that I might gain the weak: I am made all things to all men, that I might by all means save some. And this I do for the gospel's sake, that I might be partaker thereof with you. Know ye not that they which run in a race run all, but one receiveth the prize? So run, that ye may obtain.* I cannot read this chapter without making a comment on verse 24. I underscored in my Bible the two words *so run*. If someone is looking for a theme for the year, might I suggest, "so run." "So run" your ministry. "So run" your Christian life. "So run" your walk with God. "So run" your Church. "So run" your bus ministry. "So run" your nursing home ministry. "So run" your jail ministry.

Verses 25-27 says, *And every man that striveth for the mastery is temperate in all things. Now they do it to obtain a corruptible crown; but we an incorruptible. I therefore so run, not as uncertainly; so fight I, not as one that beateth the air: But I keep under my body, and bring it*

"Give Me That Old-Time Religion!"

into subjection: lest that by any means, when I have preached to others, I myself should be a castaway.

The verse I would like to emphasis is verse 27: *But I keep under my body, and bring it into subjection: lest that by any means, when I have preached to others, I myself should be a castaway.* On September 30, 1979, at the Ambassador Baptist Church in Allen Park, Michigan, I was birthed into the family of God. Two weeks later, God called me to preach. Within thirty days of being saved, I began to preach. It is an interesting fact that the churches where I was saved and surrendered to preach were both fundamental Baptist churches. A person would be correct in saying, "John N. Hamblin cut his spiritual teeth on the Old-Time Religion." For well over a quarter of a century, fundamentalism is that in which I was birthed, on which I bragged, and to which I attempted to bring others. But at this hour, I have actual consternation about certain areas of our movement. In I Corinthians Chapter 9, we find Christian liberty regarding service for Christ. Read carefully and prayerfully the twenty-seven verses that make up I Corinthians Chapter 9, because its theme, topic, thrust, and truth is again dealing with Christian liberty in our service for Christ. This chapter can be easily outlined or laid out like this:

Verses 1-23 - Christian Liberty and Paul's Approach
Verses 24-27 - Christian Liberty and Paul's Appeal

It is while the Apostle Paul is dealing under the direct inspiration of the Holy Spirit with Christian Liberty and Paul's appeal that a person gets to peek inside the heart of a Gospel preacher and perceive what was his greatest phobia. Verse 27 says, *lest that by any means, when I have preached to others, I myself should be a castaway.* Now the word *castaway* in the Greek language means "disapproved or disqualified." Dr. John R. Rice once wrote about our text, "Paul had no fear of losing his salvation, but he did fear about becoming unacceptable as a preacher."

The sister verse of I Corinthians 9:27 is Jeremiah 6:30. Every verse in the Bible has what I call a sister verse. Often that sister verse will throw more light upon the verse that we are musing, meditating, or studying. The sister verse of I Corinthians 9:27 is Jeremiah 6:30. There the Bible uses the word *reprobate*. This is a word picture; it is speaking of scraps of silver. *Reprobate silver shall men call them, because the LORD hath rejected them.* Never forget, if the apostle of the Gentiles had some real, authentic, and legitimate fears yesterday, then God's servants can have some real, authentic, and legitimate fears today. Do not miss this. It even bears repeating. If the apostle of the Gentiles had some real, authentic, and legitimate fears yesterday, then God's servants can have some real, authentic, and legitimate fears today.

Friend, those of us who are militant fundamentalists (I am not talking about milquetoast fundamentalists) ought to be in a panic at the present state of our fundamental movement! Let me say that this is not my first time around the block. In 2009, to the praise and the glory and honor of Jesus, I marked thirty years of being saved and thirty years of being in full-time evangelism. My ticket agent at Northwest tells me that the amount of my air travel last year was forty thousand plus miles, which they tell me equals going one time around the globe, going one time around the earth, going one time around the equator at the fat part of the globe and working on a quarter of a second trip. I am not a novice or a rookie. I have been at this a while. I have some concerns. I have some consternation. I have some things that absolutely terrify me about our fundamental movement.

I. Preachers without a Fullness

Luke 24:49 says, *And, behold, I send the promise of my Father upon you: but tarry ye in the city of Jerusalem, until ye be endued with power from on high.* One thing that panics me at present about our fundamental movement is preachers without a fullness. In Luke 24:49, the physician Luke tells us that one of the last things that the Lord Jesus Christ stated before He walked up that invisible stairway at His ascension was that every servant of His must have an anointing. It is extremely interesting for a person to note, that even though some of these disciples had seen miracles, stood in the shadow of Calvary, and sprinted to the empty tomb, the Saviour still plainly said to them, "Without serious tarrying, you can have no supernatural touch." Before these men could ever be

"Give Me That Old-Time Religion!"

heralders of the bodily resurrection, they must first have contact with Heaven.

A great Bible student once wrote concerning this clear command that fell from the lips of the lovely Lord Jesus Christ, "The evangelizing of a lost world demanded more than willing men with the knowledge of the written Word." He then penned, "The preacher should first learn to kneel in his upper room and only then to stand in his pulpit." I am saying there is a difference between politics and power. There is a difference between smooth games and a spiritual touch. There is a difference between organizing and having an obvious touch of Heaven upon our lives. My fear as a fundamentalist is preachers without a fullness!

> *"The preacher should first learn to kneel in his upper room and only then to stand in his pulpit."*

Friend, we ought to be afraid that in our fundamental movement we have preachers who have absolutely no clue, no idea, and no notion of what the power of God is. The Bible says in Ephesians 5:18, *And be not drunk with wine, wherein is excess; but be filled with the Spirit.* Mark it down. The modern-day curse of fundamentalism is the so-called success of far too many of our ministries that can be attributed to everything but a spirit-filled man of God. If one's ministry can be described by politics, then it is not power. If one's ministry can be described by purpose, then it is not power. If one's ministry can be described by petty games, then it is not power. I believe with all my heart that the curse of fundamentalism is that the success of many so-called ministries can be attributed to this, that, and the other when it ought to be attributed to their spirit-filled man of God.

D. L. Moody used to say, "It is a sin to do God's work without God's power." May I just for a moment throw off the spiritual boxing gloves and go at it bare fisted with each one of us? We talk about how many years we have been saved and preaching, but do we have the touch? I am glad we have been saved and preaching for a while, but do we have the touch?

My Three Fears as a Fundamentalist

We talk about all the degrees we have received in Bible college. I am not against that. I am closely connected to a Bible college. I am not against education, but all we talk about is our Bible college degrees. I have a question? Do we have the touch? I like what an evangelist said, "You can have degrees without a temperature."

We talk about Bible college degrees, but do we have the touch? We talk about going to the Holy Land and walking where Jesus walked, but do we have the touch? We talk about using only the King James Bible; and God forbid that we would use any other kind of Bible, because any other kind of Bible is not the Bible. We talk about using the King James Bible, but do we have the touch? We wear three-button suits, killer neckties, shined shoes, hankies in our outside suit pockets, and Gospel tracts in our inside suit pockets; but, do we have the touch? We do not let the smallest strand of hair touch our ears, but do we have the touch?

We do not go to the movies—or at least we should not. I have absolutely no respect for the preacher who goes to the movies. If I found out that a preacher went to the movies, I would be out of that church in a heartbeat. I would not sit under that preacher's ministry. If he slipped off and went to the movies, I would not care who he was. We do not go to the movies, but do we have the touch?

We get the *Sword of the Lord* in our mailboxes, but do we have the touch? We have Hyles', Hudson's, Roberson's, and Malone's signatures in our Bibles, but do we have the touch? We do not dance, chew, or date the girls who do, but do we have the touch? I have a fear for fundamentalism, and my fear is preachers without a fullness. Only our hearts and Heaven know the answer to that probing inquiry. Do we really have the touch?

On August 14, 2003, America experienced its most widespread, devastating, and crippling blackout. There was no power whatsoever in the Detroit area. The next day, the *Detroit Free Press* explained it like this: "The nation's worst-ever blackout, which spread across parts of seven states and Canada on Thursday and left fifty-million people powerless, could last through the weekend in Southeast Michigan." Businesses were asked to remain closed. Residents were asked to

"Give Me That Old-Time Religion!"

unplug their air conditioners on what was expected to be one of the year's hottest days. Southeastern Michigan residents who get their water from Detroit's massive water system were warned to boil water before drinking it. Detroit Metro Airport shut down Thursday evening, and it was unclear when the major Mid-Western transportation hub would reopen. That was the article. That was in the next day's paper after that great blackout, America's largest, on August 14, 2003.

But the headline that ran across that article and the top of that paper is a headline I will never forget. I have carried the headline that was on that paper with me across America. I have it in my briefcase; and every once in a while, I will pull it out and look at it. The headline read "Powerless." I am afraid that this headline could describe many pastors, evangelists, and missionaries in this country and around the world. We are powerless. We do not have the touch. We do not have the hand of God on us. We do not have the breath of God upon us. I fear, in our movement preachers without a fullness.

I could not count the number of times I have carried this newspaper across the country and have taken it out and used it as an old-fashioned altar. I put it next to my motel bed and got down on my knees and said, "Oh, God, please, please don't let this be the headline of my ministry."

Friend, if someone is reading this truth and getting angry, it is because he is powerless and he knows it. I would get down on my knees and I would beg God, "Oh, God, don't let this be the headline of my ministry. Please don't let this be the history of my walk with God. God don't let this be the description, the one word that describes my preaching." We have a problem. I fear we have preachers without a fullness. Instead of explaining it away, we should experience it. My fear as a fundamentalist is preachers without a fullness!

II. Prayers without a Fervency

James 5:16b-17 says, *The effectual fervent prayer of a righteous man availeth much. Elias was a man subject to like passions as we are, and he prayed earnestly that it might not rain.* Another thing that panics me about the present fundamental movement is prayers without a

My Three Fears as a Fundamentalist

fervency. In James 5:16-17, the servant James tells us that when a child of God is right with God, his supplication moves the very hand of God. Prayer, on the pages of the Bible, is not an effortless thing; but prayer, on the pages of the Bible, is an absolutely effective thing. This reminds a person of two important things in regard to prayer: the exhortation—*The effectual fervent prayer of a righteous man availeth much* and the example—*Elias was a man subject to like passions as we are, and he prayed earnestly that it might not rain.*

This just in: The burning prayers of a prophet, on the pages of the Bible, had the power to turn the handle to "on" or "off" on Heaven's water valve. Friend, we ought to be absolutely afraid that in our fundamental movement we have prayers without fervency! If someone doubts or debates the worth of that concern for a second, he need only to ask himself the question, "When is the last time I felt the spiritual temperature rise in the midweek prayer meeting at my church? When was the last time I felt the spiritual temperature go up half a degree in my own prayer closet?"

I have a fear, a consternation that in fundamentalism we have prayers, but we have prayers that have absolutely no fervency. We are almost experts. We can almost write a book on anything and everything. We have almost come to the place where we think that if there is not anything more we can learn, that there is not anything more that we can experience, and that there is not anything more we can get from God. God help us! I have a fear. I have a concern. I have absolute panic in my heart when we get to the place where there is absolutely no spirit, no zeal, and no temperature in our prayer lives.

I am not running for political office. I am looking to preach the truth while I am in this church. I told a young preacher the other day, "I'm not wired for politics, but I'm wired to be a prophet." There is a huge difference. God help me if I ever wet my finger to see which way the wind of popularity is blowing and then go with popularity. Friend, I would rather preach to two and tell them the truth than to preach to two thousand and compromise and capitulate and play the political game! I will not do it! People are going to be my friends because I preach the truth, not because I water it down. People are going to be my friends

"Give Me That Old-Time Religion!"

because I have a backbone and am not like a gummy bear. People are going to be my friend because they know that wherever Hamblin is, it is going to be ripping and roaring without apology. That is what it is going to be. I have got a fear. I have got a concern. I think I have been at it long enough to voice it. I think that I have been at it long enough to sound the alarm. I fear prayers without a fervency.

There are several individuals for whom the believer should be praying impassioned prayers. Now, "impassioned" is the opposite of "Lord, lay me down to sleep. I pray the Lord my soul to keep. And if I die before I wake, I pray the Lord my soul to take." Impassioned prayers are not that kind of praying. Impassioned prayers are sometimes prayers that do not even have a start, middle, or a stop. They are just constant communication with Christ—impassioned prayers.

An individual for whom the believer should be praying impassioned prayers is the sinner. Romans 10:1 says, *Brethren, my heart's desire and prayer to God for Israel is, that they might be saved.* When the children of God get back to praying for the children of the Devil with much more spiritual warmth, will be when many of them will become children of God.

At a recent *Sword of the Lord* Conference I preached on "Why I Don't Want You to Go to Hell." I remembered that, after I preached and gave an invitation, a young man came forward weeping uncontrollably. We need to see more of that. God deliver us from "altar athletes." One may ask, "What's an altar athlete?" That is someone who sprints to the altar and sprints back. If God touches a person's heart to move to the altar, he should just stay there until he knows he has gotten through to Heaven and Heaven has gotten through to him. This young man came forward weeping uncontrollably. I thought he was coming to get saved, but I later learned after the service that he was coming to pray for his lost grandfather. He came that way not only Sunday morning, but also Sunday night, Monday night, Tuesday night, Wednesday night, Thursday night, and Friday night. He came and bathed the altar with his hot, salty tears.

Saturday morning, I received a voicemail message from Dr. David Carr. He said, "Doc, I just wanted to call and tell you." He called that young man's name and said, "I just found out that he had the privilege of leading his grandfather to the Lord Jesus." Oh, Friend, would to God that we get back to that kind of praying. Would to God that we have impassioned prayers for sinners!

Other individuals for whom the believer should be praying impassioned prayers are servants. Matthew 9:38 says, *Pray ye therefore the Lord of the harvest, that he will send forth labourers into his harvest.* Now, this may come as a real revelation. The place for the church to get the workers she needs is not from another church, but from a piping hot altar. Preacher, do not eye somebody from another church. Do not say, "Boy, I wish I had him or her." Do not get your eyes on another family. God has given us the families we need. I believe that if we just began to pray for workers in our fundamental churches that we would answer our own prayers. That is why I say that the young fellows ought to have a bus route, preach in the jail, or preach in junior church. Do not just sit there and soak up services. Get plugged in and do something for Jesus.

If people started praying for bus workers at their church, God might answer that prayer by nudging that cold heart and saying, "Go get some keys." If people would start praying for altar workers at their church, God just might nudge someone's heart to answer that prayer and surrender to be an altar worker. I believe that whatever a great church needs is in that church. If we would just pray for servants, God might just touch our hearts and we might be the very answers to our own prayers. Young preachers ought to be doing something in the church. They ought to be joined with, plugged in, and doing something to lighten the load of their preacher. I do not want to know how much someone loves the man of God if he is sitting like a bump on a log doing absolutely nothing. We should love Jesus enough to get off our blessed backsides and get plugged in to the work of God, get ourselves in a ministry and do something for Jesus. What are we praying?

We ought to get off our spiritual backsides, and quit whittling at the stick of "do nothing," and sitting on the stool of "do less"! Get plugged in and do something for God. We can lighten the load of that man of God. Get a ministry. We should answer the prayer of our church and surrender to God. This church is praying for servants. The servants

"Give Me That Old-Time Religion!"

are not in another church; they are in this church. We can answer our own prayers by just praying that God will give us servants. Oh, that we pray impassioned prayers for servants.

A third individual for whom a believer should pray impassioned prayers is a stray. Luke 15:20 says, *And he arose, and came to his father. But when he was yet a great way off, his father saw him, and had compassion, and ran, and fell on his neck, and kissed him.* It is the Christian who has prayed sweltering prayers for the prodigal who will be the first one to see the prodigal start back to the Father's house. The reason the prodigals come back and we blow them out of the pew is that we have not prayed for them. That is the reason why.

I know a young man who came to hear me preach one time. He was out in the world. He was backslidden. He knew it, and God knew it. He walked in to hear me preach. Now that is wonderful. That is what we want. The young man walked in, and some stinking hag saddled up next to him, chewed him up for not being in church, and he respectfully took it. God bless him. I would not have, but he respectfully took it. Then I watched as he turned and walked out. I never had a chance to preach the Bible to him. I never had the chance to open the Word of God and let him hear it. He was on my prayer list. I invited him. I was glad that he was there. He had come to hear me preach, and somebody who certainly had not prayed for him blew him right out of the church.

A dear lady came to me with tears streaming down her cheeks. She said, "I have a prodigal." Sister, in Luke Chapter 15, the prodigal comes home. There are many great things in Luke Chapter 15. What absolutely thrills my heart is that in Luke 15, the prodigal comes back. That is how the story ends. It ends with his coming home. Friend, we ought to be praying impassioned prayers for strays! When they come back, we will be the first ones to see them.

By the way, the father saw the son before the elder brother because the father was praying for the prodigal. The elder son did not even have him on his prayer list. The elder son did not even say, "Would you pray for my brother?" The elder son was never at the altar praying for his wayward brother. Friend, we ought to be praying impassioned prayers for sinners, for servants, and for strays!

At the close of Buddy's busy day, Buddy was praying with his father. They got to the very end of the prayer and Buddy said, "...in Christ's name, Amen." Then all of a sudden, Buddy said, "Daddy, how high do our prayers go? Does God hear us when we pray?"

The father, loving the challenge of answering the questions that sons often give, said, "Yes, Son, God hears everything, and God heard our prayer tonight." Buddy smiled and slipped off to sleep. But the father stayed up many hours wondering, "How high do my prayers go?" I have come to say to each and every one of us that I have it on good authority that hot prayers go high, all the way to Heaven, all the way to the throne. God hears and answers hot prayers. I am concerned. I have consternation about prayers without a fervency!

III. Programs without a Fundamental Foundation

Proverbs 22:28 says, *Remove not the ancient landmark, which thy fathers have set.* A thing that panics me at the present with our fundamental movement is programs without a fundamental foundation. In Proverbs 22:28, the wise man Solomon tells us about the authoritative landmarks, marked-with-age milestones that are not to be moved, not even a millimeter, from where they have been anchored. To feel the full weight of that verse, one must understand that in the lands of the Middle East, dishonest people would often move the series of stones which indicated the boundaries of the farmer's property to increase the size of their property at their neighbor's expense. Spiritually, it deals with those series of markers which are orthodox doctrines and duties as well as the mandates and methods of fundamental Christianity. Friend, we ought to be afraid that, in our fundamental movement, we have programs that seemingly mean nothing, that do not have a fundamental foundation.

The Bible says in Jude 3, *Beloved, when I...exhort you that ye should earnestly contend for the faith which was once delivered unto the saints.* Those two words *the faith* used in that verse do not mean that you are coming to Christ." Those two words *the faith* found in Jude 3 are talking about the entire, the whole body of truth. That is what it means. Christian, we are in need of a spiritual "seeing-eye dog" if we cannot observe

"Give Me That Old-Time Religion!"

that in some of our fundamental corners there are mission programs, colleges, preachers, and meetings that are being promoted, supported, and advertised that not only have the scent of new evangelicalism on them, but also are not even a shadow of the faith once delivered unto the saints. The term *new evangelicalism* is fundamentalism that went to the movies. New evangelicalism is fundamentalism that is backslidden. New evangelicalism is fundamentalism that would not know separation if it stood in the middle of the road with a Goodyear blimp flying over it shouting, "That's separation." There are mission programs, preachers, and colleges that are not even a shadow of the faith once delivered unto the saints.

While preparing this message, I was thinking about how I needed an illustration that would drive home the point beyond any shadow of a doubt. I began to think, and it crossed my mind that there is a legend that bears mentioning. The Trojan War had raged on for many years, and there seemed to be no end in sight. The two sides, the Greeks and the Trojans were in battle over Helen, the most beautiful woman in the world. She had originally been Helen of Sparta; but, because she was so attractive, Paris of Troy decided to carry her off. Helen, that was who the whole battle was over, that was who the whole fight was over. It was all over Helen. Since the Greeks knew that they could not win by force, they decided to win by trickery. A few of the men hid themselves in a huge, hollow wooden horse. I have read where some scholars of Greek mythology have guessed that there were anywhere from ten to fifty soldiers in that huge, hollow wooden horse. I do not know the exact number, but it would have to be closer to fifty than it would be ten because of what happened. Since the Greeks knew they would not be able to win by force, they got that hollow wooden horse, known as the Trojan horse, and put ten to fifty soldiers in it. The rest packed up in their ship and left. One Greek named Sinon went into Troy as a spy. The Trojans thought that the Greeks had surrendered and were persuaded by Sinon to bring the horse into the city as a victory trophy. That night, the soldiers came out of the horse and opened the gates of Troy. The Greek ships that had been waiting out beyond the horizon came and ransacked Troy, and thus the war was ended. From the story comes the

My Three Fears as a Fundamentalist

old adage, "Beware of Greeks bearing gifts." We had better stop listening to the spiritual spies with the name of Sinon who have infiltrated our fundamental churches, who are trying to get us to go outside the house of God, who are trying to get us to go outside of the body, trying to get us to go outside of fundamentalism and drag in Troy's Trojan horse so that it will destroy us.

That is why the young preachers ought to be plugged in. Whether they realize it or not, there is coming a day when the baton is going to be in their hands. If they are not serious now, they are never going to be serious. If they are playing now, they will forever play. If it is just a game, something they would like to be around and not in, then they will forever be that way.

The older I get, the greater the burden, the greater the weight, and the greater the seriousness that we have all around us. Outside the walls of our fundamental churches are a hoard and a host of spiritual Trojan horses and spiritual Sinons who are in the house of God. The only way to cure the problem is to spiritually cut off their heads. That is the only way to cure that. They are saying, "Bring in the bad music. Bring in the preacher. Although he is a fundamentalist this week, he's a new evangelical most of the other times. Bring in the preacher who sneaks off to the movies." I do not care if it harelips the Pope. No preacher has any business going to the movies.

A friend of mine said, "Hamblin is a warrant officer of preachers."

I said, "If preachers acted right, I wouldn't have to be the warrant officer." What he meant as a criticism, I took as a compliment. Apparently, he was upset about something. Outside the doors of our churches are these spiritual Trojan horses, bad music, preachers who flip-flop, preachers who one never knows where they stand, and preachers and singing groups who are not separated.

I have been at this long enough to sound the alarm. Music is killing us. There is a balance between crazy contemporary and stuff I hear at funerals. It is okay if it has a beat, because my heart has one. It does not have to be dead and dry. It does not have to remind us of a funeral. I am for class, but I am for camp meeting, too. I believe we can

"Give Me That Old-Time Religion!"

have both. We are letting folks come in to our churches who we ought not let come in because they are spiritual Trojan horses. They are going to destroy the fundamentalism that we have. They are going to ruin it for the next generation. We have those Trojan horses of literature that have bad Bible verses in them. *Daily Bread* ought not to be in a fundamental church. We should not be supporting *Samaritan's Purse*. We should not be taking people to Billy Graham Crusades. All of these are Spiritual Trojan horses that a Sinon is trying to get us to drag into the house of God, and they will ruin us in the long run.

Paul said he had a fear. He said, *But I keep under my body, and bring it into subjection: lest that by any means, when I have preached to others, I myself should be a castaway* (I Corinthians 9:27). If he could have a fear, I think I can, too. A weak stand on the King James Bible is a Trojan horse.

I told a fellow the other day, "You made a statement in my presence the other day, and I didn't appreciate it."

He said, "What did I say?"

I said, "You said that as long as we fire the gun, we don't need to defend the gun. Sir, a statement like that is modernism. If we don't defend the Bible, there will be no Bible to use." I did not ask him if he liked it or not. I have been at this long enough to voice some of my fears. The days of my being quiet are all gone. There is a generation behind us, and I think they deserve what I have enjoyed. I think they deserve what I have experienced.

Chapter Six

When God Gets in a Killing Mood

I John 5:16-17 says, *If any man see his brother sin a sin which is not unto death, he shall ask, and he shall give him life for them that sin not unto death. There is a sin unto death: I do not say that he shall pray for it. All unrighteousness is sin...* I cannot read that phrase without making some type of a comment. *All unrighteousness is sin!* That is not tithing, gossiping, a bad attitude, and staying out of church! The verse I would like to emphasize is I John 5:16: *If any man see his brother sin a sin which is not unto death, he shall ask, and he shall give him life for them that sin not unto death. There is a sin unto death: I do not say that he shall pray for it.* If my count is correct, there is in this verse a six-word phrase. With the help of God, I would like to try to lift and lay upon each and every heart the phrase, *There is a sin unto death.*

It may seem like a startling statement to some, but it is completely scriptural. At this moment, there are death certificates filed in the filing cabinets of a celestial city, where it asks the cause of death, the answer is sin! In I John Chapter 5, we find God is life, victory over the world, and the assurance of salvation. Now, this is one of those chapters that does not have just one truth that runs the length and breadth of it; but it is one of a myriad of chapters that has several truths, and thoroughly and truthfully deals with those truths. So, if we were to take the time before

"Give Me That Old-Time Religion!"

we pillow our heads to go back to I John Chapter 5, and read these twenty-one verses, we would find that the topic is three-fold: it deals with "God is life," "victory over the world," and "assurance of salvation." This chapter can be easily outlined or laid out like this:

> Verses 1-5 - The Test
> Verses 6-15 - The Testimonies
> Verses 16-17 - The Two Transgressions
> Verse 18 - The Touch
> Verses 19-21 - The Truth

It is while the Apostle John is dealing under the direct inspiration of the Holy Spirit with the two transgressions that a person reads one of the most startling, sobering, and scary verses in all of the Scriptures, verse 16: *If any man see his brother sin a sin which is not unto death, he shall ask, and he shall give him life for them that sin not unto death. There is a sin unto death: I do not say that he shall pray for it.*

I read where Evangelist Oliver B. Greene once wrote about our text, "When a Christian falls into sin and continues to live in known sin, refusing to repent, such living will bring physical death." I am afraid that there are many people in and out of the church who live like this verse is not in their Bible. But, this verse is in the inspired and preserved Bible. It is in the Bible of Heaven and in the Bible of earth. *There is a sin unto death.* Friend, those who are saved and unsaved must know that sometimes the God of Heaven "bumps people off!" There are at least three different sins of which we should make a mental note that brings slaughter. There are at least three different sins that put God in a killing mood.

I. When We Try to Steal God's Majesty

Acts 12:23 says, *And immediately the angel of the Lord smote him, because he gave not God the glory: and he was eaten of worms, and gave up the ghost.* A sin that will put God in a killing mood is when we try to steal God's majesty. Herod was a politician and an orator. The Bible tells us in Acts Chapter 12 that one day Herod sits upon his throne,

When God Gets in a Killing Mood

arrayed in all of his kingly vesture; and as he is on that throne, he gives this oration. I believe that he was Churchill and Tallmadge rolled up into one. He had the ability of painting pictures with words. He had the ability of playing marbles on the coattails of comets. So Herod sits upon his throne arrayed in all this kingly finery. He gives this oration, and when he gets done the people immediately shout, *It is the voice of a god and not of a man.* Then, God strikes him! Then, God hits him! Then, God kills him graveyard dead! Herod tried to take the honor, majesty, and glory that only belong to a Holy God! God gets in a killing mood when we try to steal God's majesty! It does not matter if people are moved by our speech, song, or sermon. When they compliment us, we need to immediately give God glory in our hearts. The Bible says in Psalm 115:1, *Not unto us, O LORD, not unto us, but unto thy name give glory...*

Since I was a boy, I have always had a great fascination with the *Titanic.* I have numbers of books in my study on the *Titanic.* I have a scale model of the *Titanic* that someone built for me. I have a piece of coal that was retrieved from the floor of the North Atlantic. The *Titanic* burned six hundred and fifty tons of coal per day. I have in my study a copy of the New York paper that had the right headline that the *Titanic* had sunk. The first headline said that the ship had struck an iceberg but that everything was all right and she was limping her way to New York, but that was not the case. I have a copy, not the original, but a copy of the first right headline of a New York paper. I have a penny from the very year that the *Titanic* sank, 1912. Recently someone gave me an artist rendering of the *Titanic* leaving Queenstown signed by the last living survivor, Milvina Dean. (She just passed on.) I have always been a student of the *Titanic* and fascinated by the *Titanic.* I think that it is a good thing for a preacher to have in his office *Titanic* memorabilia that reminds him not to get a big head, to think he is something, to try to sail and steam ahead on his own. I think it is a good idea! A second-class passenger, Mrs. Albert Coldwell, asked a deck hand, "Is this ship really unsinkable?" That deck hand said, "Yes, not even God could sink the *Titanic.*" The *Titanic* was the very first ship that ever had water on the inside. It had a pool. It is the very first ship that ever had water on the inside on purpose. Listen to that deck hand again as he said to Mrs.

Coldwell, "Yes, Lady, God Himself could not sink this ship." But on April 14, 1912, just a few moments before midnight, the *Titanic* struck an iceberg. Then on April 15, 1912, the *Titanic* went to her watery grave, and 1,502 people perished and went into eternity all because time should not steal God's majesty!

II. When We Try to Stand against God's Man

Numbers 16:32 says, *And the earth opened her mouth, and swallowed them up, and their houses, and all the men that appertained unto Korah, and all their goods.* There is a sin that puts God in a killing mood, and that is when we try to stand against God's man! In Numbers Chapter 16, Moses tells us how Korah and his crowd stood up against him. This was rebellion against Moses' leadership. What Korah and his crowd said was, "Moses and Aaron, you take too much upon yourselves." God did not like that! Just imagine stepping in the time machine of the Bible and going back to the book of Numbers. Stand in the shadows of that city as Korah rose up against the man of God, and as he attacked the man of God, and the man of God's family.

When we go against the preacher, we go against his family. If we come against the man of God, against his precious wife, and his dear children, God help our backslidden heart! Sometimes people will get upset with the preacher, and they will attack his family. They will not attack him personally, but will attack his family. If we get angry at the man of God, we should have enough guts and gumption to take it out on him and not attack his wife or his children. If someone were to do that to me, I may not act like I am a great Christian. When someone attacks my family, we are going behind the church, and we are going to forget about this reverend business, and we are going to boogie without music.

Just imagine going back in the time machine of the Scripture to the shadow of this scene. Korah says, "Now Moses, you just take way too much upon yourself." But wait a minute. Something happens. The earth begins to shake and quake. I wish I had been there. Someone may ask me, "Why would you want to be there?" To shout! It is about time rebels get their reward. I would have loved to have been there. All of a sudden

When God Gets in a Killing Mood

the earth begins to shake and quake. The earth opens up, and Korah and that crowd, their houses, and goods go down to Hell. Go ahead and cause trouble in the church. Go ahead and split the church, but there is still a God in Heaven Who gets in a killing mood!

In another account of the same scene in Numbers 26:10, God says, *and they became a sign.* I looked up that word *sign* in my Strong's Concordance and it means, "a banner." When we think about causing trouble and standing against the man of God, look at the banner of the Bible and hear God say to us, "You may do it if you wish, but I may kill you if I want because there is a banner." If someone wants to cause trouble in the church, attack the preacher, or rise up against the man of God, then God gets in a killing mood.

There are some safeguards to prevent us from committing this sin. Trying to stand against God's man is a sin. It is just as much a sin as getting drunk. It is just as much a sin as putting dope in one's veins. It is just as much a sin as stealing hubcaps, refrigerators, or DVD players.

First of all, a safeguard that will keep us from this sin as a saint is submitting to preachers. Hebrews 13:17, *Obey them...* We do not need fifteen commentaries on the Bible to understand that! *Obey them that have the rule over you, and submit yourselves: for they watch for your souls, as they that must give account, that they may do it with joy, and not with grief: for that is unprofitable for you.*

One may say, "Well, I submit to him when he tells me to call on my class as a Sunday school teacher. I submit to him when he gives me the Sunday school literature that I should use as a Sunday school teacher. I submit to him as a choir director when he says, 'This modern music is not even to be sung in our restrooms.' I submit to him when he says that we should not have choir practice before the evening service but before Sunday school because our service ought to have somewhat of a sacrifice to it. If we are going to sing then we should sacrifice before we sing."

But when he says, "Now Sunday school needs to end ten minutes before the morning service," and we say, "My spiritual lesson is so good that I need to run five minutes after," then we are not obeying. Half

"Give Me That Old-Time Religion!"

obedience is full rebellion. Do we want to commit the sin where God kills us?

A second safeguard for a saint to keep from committing a sin is to supplicate for preachers. Hebrews 13:18 says, *Pray for us: for we trust we have a good conscience, in all things willing to live honestly.* I know when people do not pray for me because they argue with me. I know when people do not pray for me because they oppose me. I am not infallible, but I am God's man. I make no apology for it. I am not "going to be" God's man or in a program where one day I will achieve and be God's man; no, I am God's man. When someone is cranky and irritable and does not get along with the man of God that is a good indicator that he is not praying for the man of God. When was the last time that we prayed for our preacher? I did not ask when was the last time that we criticized him. We are saying we do not pray for the man of God when we criticize him. Supplicate for the man of God.

A third safeguard that will keep a saint from this sin is saluting every preacher. Hebrews 13:24 says, *Salute all them that have the rule over you, and all the saints. They of Italy salute you.* This word *salute* means to "enfold in the arms." Paul said to *salute all*. That means young preachers, too. What we are supposed to do is enfold them in our arms. It is hard to fight with somebody when we are holding him in our arms. It is hard to hit someone when we are holding him. All we can do when we are holding him is hold him. The reason we beat up on preachers or that we try to is that we are not holding them in our arms. The reason people get upset, quarrel, and fight with preachers is that they are not saluting them, or enfolding them in their arms. Oh, that every saint would realize that the safeguards that will keep us from committing this sin is submitting to preachers, supplicating for preachers, and saluting many preachers!

I heard my mentor, Dr. Tom Malone, Sr. tell the story about Dr. John R. Rice being invited to preach at a revival meeting. The pastor got up and said, "Now in five weeks Dr. Rice is coming. We have the privilege of having the Twentieth Century's mightiest pen, the editor of the *Sword of the Lord*. He will be preaching for us in a revival meeting." It happened to be in a Southern Baptist Church that was coming out of the

Southern Baptist Convention. The preacher made the announcement; and after the service, a deacon pulled him aside and said, "I want to understand you right. Did you say that Dr. Rice is coming to have a revival meeting?"

The pastor said, "Yes. I can't believe we have him coming. What a privilege of ours!"

The deacon said, "Oh no, not Dr. Rice. He is against modernism and liberalism. He is against the Southern Baptist Convention. You can't get an edition of the *Sword of the Lord* without him firing his gun at the Convention. He is not coming here."

The pastor said, "Oh yes he is!"

The deacon said, "Over my dead body, he is coming here."

I heard Dr. Malone tell that the Saturday prior to the first service of that meeting, when the plane that carried Dr. Rice landed in the city where that meeting was to be held, that deacon fell over dead! They had his funeral in the church. Hanging over the choir loft was the banner with the revival meeting dates and Dr. John R. Rice, evangelist. God gets in a killing mood when we try to stand against God's man!

III. When We Try to Skip God's Method

II Samuel 6:7 says, *And the anger of the LORD was kindled against Uzzah; and God smote him there for his error; and there he died by the ark of God.* A sin that will put God in the killing mood is when we try to skip God's method. In II Samuel Chapter 6, the prophet Samuel tells us that David goes to move the Ark of the Covenant. He has gotten the Ark from the Philistines. It had been in the Philistine's hands. Now David goes to move it. He is so excited about it that he makes an error. David thinks, "Well, I will just move the Ark the way the Philistines did. I'll just move the Ark the way the world says to move it." But the Word of God tells us how to do the work of God. In Numbers 7:9, there are detailed instructions on how that Ark was to be moved. A person cannot just pick it up! A person was not supposed to get a cart and use it to move the Ark. Only certain people using poles could carry that Ark! David tried to do a good thing in a bad way. David put the Ark on a new cart. I am sorry, David. I know David is the sweet Psalmist of Israel, and that

"Give Me That Old-Time Religion!"

he is the man after God's own heart, but David is dead wrong! He puts the Ark on a new cart. He began to move it and it starts to shake. Uzzah reaches out to steady the Ark. God kills him! What did David do? He tried to skip God's method.

I know of churches that when the Super Bowl comes, they get some big screen TV and put it in the auditorium. Then they have a five-minute devotion. Why bring the Bible into that? They have a five-minute devotion, and then they have a chili cook-off in the fellowship hall. Then the church watches the Super Bowl. I am not being crude, but I wonder what they did during the half-time show? When a church just absolutely stops having Sunday night church services, stresses teaching over preaching, succumbs to a praise team instead of a choir, and signs off on everything that is fundamental, they step off the old paths. The Bible says in Jeremiah 6:16 *...and ask for the old paths, where is the good way, and walk therein...*

> *When a church just absolutely stops having Sunday night church services, stresses teaching over preaching, succumbs to a praise team instead of a choir, and signs off on everything that is fundamental, they step off the old paths.*

Some years ago, I had the privilege of visiting Mount Hermon School for Boys. It is a forerunner of the Christian school. The founder of Mount Hermon was Dwight Lyman Moody. It is amazing that a preacher, even without an education, would create an institution of education. Mr. Moody had started Mount Hermon. If one were to go to Mount Hermon today, he would see things that really would make a stone weep. They play rock music out of the dormitories. The same buildings where D.L. Moody's song leader, Ira Sanky once sang, Satan now sings. While I was there, I went into the bookstore and I picked up a book by Burnham Carter called *So Much to Learn*. It was written for the 100th commemoration of Mount Hermon.

I was holding a revival meeting in New England, and I picked up that book and I went back to my motel room and vowed to God that I would not stop reading until I found the place where Mount Hermon made the turn. I read for several hours that afternoon, and then read again after the services were over until about 3 a.m. At 3 a.m., I found it. In the book, I learned about Elliot Sphere. Elliot Sphere was the president at Mount Hermon. He felt some pressure from the faculty and the students, so he loosened up the rules. Now D. L. Moody started Mount Hermon. Someone asked Mr. Moody, "If someone smokes will they go to Hell?" Mr. Moody said, "No, if they are saved, they don't go to Hell; they will just smell like they have been there." Here is a president of Moody's school putting a smoking room for the faculty. They called it the "blue cloud." That is not all. He brought in teachers from the Arthur Murray School of Dance. They taught the students and faculty how to dance. Someone may ask, "What's wrong with dancing?" We should wipe off the dust from our Bibles and ask John the Baptist what is wrong with dancing! Elliot Sphere was a modernist, a wolf in sheep's clothing. He was a liberal! It is very, very, very interesting that in 1932 Elliot Sphere was murdered. To this day, no one knows who the killer was. To this day, his murder is shrouded in mystery! But Elliot Sphere, while he was president of Mount Hermon became graveyard dead.

  I have in my hand an envelope that a friend gave to me. It is a death certificate. It is issued when somebody dies. I have a death certificate, a state of Michigan department of community health certificate of death. There is a number in the corner that says 2414781. This is the real deal. It has a section that says, "Manner of death: accident, suicide, homicide, natural, intermediate or pending specification." There is a blank that a doctor can fill in that says what killed the person. Christian, there are some sins that will put God in a killing mood! What will the Great Physician fill in on your death certificate where it states "manner of death"?

"Give Me That Old-Time Religion!"

Chapter Seven

Please, Let Me Preach Your Funeral

Genesis 50:22-26 says, *And Joseph dwelt in Egypt, he, and his father's house: and Joseph lived an hundred and ten years. And Joseph saw Ephraim's children of the third generation: the children also of Machir the son of Manasseh were brought up upon Joseph's knees. And Joseph said unto his brethren, I die: and God will surely visit you, and bring you out of this land unto the land which he sware to Abraham, to Isaac, and to Jacob. And Joseph took an oath of the children of Israel, saying, God will surely visit you, and ye shall carry up my bones from hence. So Joseph died, being an hundred and ten years old: and they embalmed him, and he was put in a coffin in Egypt.* Please look back with me at verse 26. I thought about putting in my Bible, next to the word *coffin*, the words *hope chest*. That is what a coffin is for a child of God, a hope chest.

As a preacher of the Gospel for more than a quarter of a century, I have been asked to conduct a considerable number of memorial services. Nowhere between the covers of the written voice of God is a man of God commanded to marry or bury. He has been given the green light from Heaven to select which one of these services he wants to perform. Through the years, I have been asked to speak at the memorial services of family, friends, and faithful servants of God. Not one time did I ever request these observances, but was requested. On the other

"Give Me That Old-Time Religion!"

hand, there are some caskets that I would volunteer to stand at the head of and voice the grand news of that person's passing. "Please, let me preach your funeral." In Genesis Chapter 50, we find the last days and deaths of the patriarchs Jacob and Joseph. This chapter can be easily outlined or laid out like this:

> Verses 1-13 - Burying the Beloved Father
> Verses 14-21 - Burying a Past
> Verses 22-26 - Burying a Devoted Brother

It is while the prophet Moses is dealing under the direct inspiration of the Holy Spirit with burying a devoted brother that the person is given a chair in the funeral parlor of a great servant of God. Verse 26, *So Joseph died, being an hundred an ten years old: and they embalmed him, and he was put in a coffin in Egypt.* The Bible is a practical handbook on burials. It covers everything from burial sites (Genesis 23:1-20), funeral processions (Genesis 50:7-9), significance of burials (II Samuel 2:4-6), funeral music (Matthew 9:23-24), and burials of saved individuals (Acts 8:2). An individual must keep in the forefront of his mind, that so much care was taken in Ancient Egypt to embalm the body; there were many who were buried without coffins. The mention of the fact that Joseph was put in a coffin shows the high rank to which he had attained. His coffin was probably an outside receptacle. Whether it was of wood or of stone, we have no means of knowing. Stone material would probably be used for such an exalted person. Never forget, while most services tend to cause a saint to shed a tear, there are memorial services that would truly cause a servant of God to shout. Do not miss that statement. It bears repeating. While most memorial services tend to cause a saint of God to shed a tear, there are some memorial services that would truly cause a servant of God to shout. Friend, those of us who are saved need to hear about the funerals a preacher would step forward to preach. Now again, in more than a quarter of a century of preaching, I have never requested to preach anyone's funeral, but there are some funerals that upon my heart, I would readily step forward; I

Please, Let Me Preach Your Funeral

would readily volunteer; I would readily say, "Please, please, please let me preach your funeral."

I. The Funeral of Mr. Disbelief

Numbers 13:31 says, *But the men that went up with him said, We be not able to go up against the people; for they are stronger than we.* A memorial service that a man of God would gladly volunteer to speak at is the funeral of "Mr. Disbelief." In this verse, the prophet Moses tells us about the negative report the ten spies gave about the land of Canaan in Kadesh-Barnea. Two spies, Caleb and Joshua, told the prophets, *Let us go up at once, and possess it.* Ten spies told the people, *We be not able to go up against the people, for they are stronger than we.* Here is an excellent rule to follow. The majority report is usually not the Master's report. It does not matter what the majority says, it only matters what the Master says. Their words dripped with cynicism and skepticism; not even a zealous new convert sitting on the front row of his first-ever emotionally charged camp meeting would holler "Amen" to their estimation of the situation. The problem is easy to detect. They forgot about . . . *surely it floweth with milk and honey* . . . in verse 27. They focused in on . . . *and all the people that we saw in it are men of a great stature* in verse 32. I was thinking that one is either a verse 27 Christian or a verse 32 Christian. One is either the Christian who says . . . *surely, it floweth with milk and honey*, or he is the kind of Christian who says . . . *and all the people . . . are men of great stature.* The difference between verse 27 and verse 32 is as different as night and day.

It was Winston Churchill who once said, "The pessimist sees difficulty in every opportunity; the opportunist sees the opportunity in every difficulty." Whenever a child of God puts more of an emphasis on the Devil's problems and not the Saviour's provisions, he will always end up placing a huge question mark over

> *Whenever a child of God puts more of an emphasis on the Devil's problems and not the Saviour's provisions, he will always end up placing a huge question mark over everything that God wants him to do for Him!*

"Give Me That Old-Time Religion!"

everything that God wants him to do for Him! I believe the work of God is overrun with Christians who say, *"and all the people . . . are men of great stature."* God, give us absolutely a resolute number of Christians who are not saying that, but are saying, *"surely it floweth with milk and honey."* Friend, we need to know that a memorial service that a man of God would gladly volunteer to preach is the funeral of "Mr. Disbelief."

The Bible says in Matthew 17:20, *...If ye have faith as a grain of mustard seed, ye shall say unto this mountain, Remove hence to yonder place; and it shall remove; and nothing shall be impossible unto you.* The mustard seed is the smallest seed known in the Lord Jesus Christ's day. If one has only a mustard seed-sized faith in his heart, he will never have in his wallet a spiritual drivers license with the name, "Mr. Disbelief" on it. It is "Mr. Disbelief" who says to every daring project of faith that the pastor attempts to lead the church to do, "I just don't think we have the money or the manpower to ever do that." In the history of the church, we have never had the money, or the manpower to do what we do. We do not count the men, or the money, and decide we are going to do it; we do not count what is in the bank account, or count noses and decide we are going to do it. We get something from God. God puts it in our heart. We get the vision. We get the goal. We get the faith to do something. Manpower and money have not one wit to do with the work of God. This is the work of an eternal God.

We do not look to manpower or money to accomplish what God places upon our heart to do. It is "Mr. Disbelief" who says, "Oh, we can't do that. We just don't have the manpower. We just don't have the money." When he talks to others about their lost loved ones being saved, he can always be counted on to give a hundred reasons why they will never trust Christ. He can always be counted on to say, "Well it's this, that, or the other. They'll never be saved." That is just the makeup, the nature, and the spiritual DNA of "Mr. Disbelief." He will always be the one that mentions that the choir had two members missing last Sunday, even though it was that same Sunday that ten first-time visitors were birthed into the family of God. If a person concentrates on empty chairs and not full altars, he is a backslider! He is looking at the wrong thing. He is observing the wrong thing. He has his eyes on the wrong thing.

Please, Let Me Preach Your Funeral

I know it is not that appropriate. I know that I am supposed to wait until they ask, but I want to volunteer. Please, please let me preach "Mr. Disbelief's" funeral.

I read that the Northwestern University Wildcats shocked the world of college football in 1995 by making it to the Rose Bowl Tournament. The man behind the team's unbelievable turnaround was Coach Gary Barnett. He was determined to prove that kids at the Big Ten's smallest and most academically demanding school could play football. He ordered a Tournament of Roses' flag for the football building and kept a silk rose on his desk to remind them where they were headed. "At the first meeting," says kicker Sam Dallas, "he told us we needed to believe without evidence. He asked, 'Do you know what that is?' And then the coach answered his inquiry and said, 'That is faith.'" It always has been and always will be fatalism that keeps many believers out of the Promised Land and many believers from the spiritual "Tournament of Roses." Let me preach the funeral of "Mr. Disbelief"!

II. The Funeral of Mrs. Division

Philippians 4:2 says, *I beseech Euodias, and beseech Syntyche, that they be of the same mind in the Lord.* A memorial service that a man of God would gladly volunteer to speak at is the funeral of "Mrs. Division." Here, the Apostle Paul tells us how that, in the church of Philippi, there were two saved females that had a falling out with each other. The name *Euodias* means "prosperous journey." The name *Syntyche* means "pleasant acquaintance." I was thinking it would be wonderful if some "pleasant acquaintances" took a "prosperous journey"!

Evangelist Oliver B. Greene once wrote about Euodias and Syntyche that the division between them had been caused by "something trivial." It is never anything major; it is always something minor. It is never something big; it is always something little. Dr. Greene said that very likely the division between them had been caused by something trivial. Perhaps one was preferred over the other, praised a bit more than the other, or perhaps one was given a position that the other thought she should have. I cannot read Philippians 4:2 without seeing in the theater of my mind Syntyche on one side trying to rally the church, and Euodias

"Give Me That Old-Time Religion!"

on the other side trying to rally the church, and that church being just a few short days from a major split. This is a preacher's nightmare. When "Mrs. Division" rises up and reigns supreme, it is a problem. It is a serious scenario because always, when "Mrs. Division" is present, there will be heartbreak and havoc in the house of God. Friend, we need to know that a memorial service a man of God would gladly volunteer to preach, is the funeral of "Mrs. Division"!

It is "Mrs. Division" who says to church members all the time, "If you don't get mad at that sister in Christ, because I'm mad at her, I will be mad at you." That is crazy. That is insane. That is absolutely absurd! I am glad that for over a quarter of a century, I have had a policy that there are three things nobody ever talks to me about: what I preach, where I preach, and who my friends are going to be. When anybody tries to put pressure on me to not like somebody, not fellowship with somebody, or as a preacher, not preach for somebody; I just mark it down, I am going to like him, fellowship with him, and preach for him. I have made a ministry out of preaching in places where I have been told not to preach. It is "Mrs. Division" who sows discord. It is "Mrs. Division" who tries to divide and bring destruction to the body of Christ.

When she attends a service, it is always to see whom she can offend or by whom she may be offended. I think there are people who come to the house of God with their feelings hanging out everywhere, and they are just looking to be offended or upset. They remind me of a spiritual Mount Rushmore. They have a chip on their shoulder and are just daring somebody to knock that chip off. Friend, listen, we ought to come to the house of God with a decision and with the determination that we are not going to be offended, put out, or miffed by anything. Here is what really drives me nuts. Somebody gets miffed, but I do not get miffed; but he wants me to be miffed because he is miffed. I am not going to let his bad attitude, bad demeanor, or bad spirit ruin my parade. I am not going to do it! In fact, if he puts any pressure on me about that, I am going to have a better time than he is having. One can be certain that "Mrs. Division" will lead the opposition against the pastor's new push for church growth. May I say again, please, please, please let me preach "Mrs. Division's" funeral.

Please, Let Me Preach Your Funeral

> *Fundamental churches just do not divide by accident; they are divided by an agenda.*

There are several different things that will divide a fundamental church. Fundamental churches just do not divide by accident; they are divided by an agenda. It just does not happen. The church just does not one Sunday become divided or separated. It just does not become one Sunday in disunity. I like what Dr. Curtis Hutson once said, "There's a vast difference between union and unity. Take two tomcats, tie them by the tail, and throw them over a clothesline, and you have union, but you don't have unity." Division does not happen by accident. That just does not happen overnight. It is not happenstance. There are some destructive things that will divide a fundamental church.

A destructive thing that will divide a church is animosity. Luke 15:28 says, *And he was angry, and would not go in...* Believers are in bad shape when their bitterness keeps them out of the choir, Sunday school class, and the church services. One may say, "Well, I'm mad at so and so. I'm not going to sing in the choir. Well I'm mad at so and so. I'm not going to sit in their Sunday school class. Well I'm mad at so and so. I'm not going to go to church." Hey, Einstein, that is not intelligent. One can hurt himself spiritually because of somebody else. It is animosity that keeps people from the choir, from the Sunday school class, and from the church. The prodigal's other brother, who was a prodigal too, said, "I will not go in." He hated his own brother. It divided that family. Animosity divides the family of God in the local church. Animosity will separate, destroy an assembly, and bring division.

A second thing that will divide a fundamental church is arrogance. Mark 10:37, *They said unto him, Grant unto us that we may sit, one on thy right hand, and the other on thy left hand, in thy glory.* Instead of a person thinking he deserves a seat on the platform like the early disciples, he needs to understand that he deserves to be in the burning pits of Hell with his back broken. That is what he really deserves. We do not deserve a seat on the platform. We deserve a place in Hell. That is what we deserve.

"Give Me That Old-Time Religion!"

This incident shocked me when it happened. I was holding a revival meeting in a distant city. One night a friend of mine came to hear me preach in that area. After the service he and I spoke, and then he left in a hurry. When I got back to the motel room that night, there was a light flashing on the phone. I retrieved the voicemail from the motel room. It was this preacher. He said, "Doc, when you get a chance give me call. There's something that I need to talk to you about." So, even though it was late, I returned his call. When he answered the phone and heard it was me, he said, "I've got a problem."

I mean right at the very beginning of the conversation he said, "I've got a problem." Man, I thought we had a great service. I mean, there were people saved. Christians got right with God. We had a tremendous crowd.

This preacher said to me, "I've got a problem."

I said, "Well my brother, what is your problem? I thought we had a wonderful service. What's the problem?"

He said, "My problem is that the preacher knew I was a preacher, and he did not ask me to pray."

I said, "If you thought that you should've prayed, I'm glad that he didn't ask you. You have no business praying."

That is nothing less than arrogance. Someone may say, "Well, I picked up a piece of paper, and you know, they didn't dedicate the church bulletin to me." "Well, I changed 42 diapers during one service in the revival meeting because Hamblin preached so long, and they didn't pat me on the back." "Well, I sang a special, but no one complimented me." We are not in this thing for us. We are in this for others, and we are especially in this thing for Him! It absolutely blows my mind how much arrogance that surfaces in the house of God. We ought to know a whole lot better than that. It is arrogance that will separate an assembly.

I was in a meeting recently. I was not trying to play or pretend to be humble. I just meant it from my heart. I met with a group of preachers to pray before the service. I found myself praying in front of them something that I usually pray by myself. I do not usually pray in front of anybody, and I was not pretending or presuming to be humble; but I was just praying with them and forgot I was with them. I found myself

Please, Let Me Preach Your Funeral

saying, "Lord, I'm just absolutely stunned. I'm absolutely shocked that I'm here, Lord. I can't even imagine anybody inviting me anywhere to do anything let alone preach. That's exactly how I feel about it. Thank You for having me. You could have anybody. Thank You for having me." If I were invited to clean the restrooms, it would be an honor. If I were invited to sing [that ain't gonna happen] but if I were, that would really be an honor. If I were invited to just run the bus and pick up people and drive them to the revival meeting, that is more than I deserve. If I got what I deserved, I would be burning in Hell with my back broken. It seems like the work of God is absolutely overrun with arrogance. That is why assemblies are separated, and churches are divided.

The third thing that will divide a fundamental church is argument. I Corinthians 1:11 says, *For it hath been declared unto me of you, my brethren, by them which are of the house of Chloe, that there are contentions among you.* By the time a believer gets out of the fifth grade, he should be past bush-league altercations at the house of God. People watch us. People listen to us. I mean, if someone is going to talk to somebody or deal with something; and there will be times that happens, go in a closed room somewhere! Post somebody at the door so that an unbeliever or a weak Christian does not walk in and be absolutely destroyed spiritually, because of someone else's lack of control. It is argument that separates and divides a church. Everyone needs to realize that the destructive things that would divide an assembly every time are animosity, arrogance, and argument!

A crowd of people at the Franklin Park Zoo in Boston watched a peacock slowly spread its large tail and display its beautiful plumage. The bird held itself erect and strutted regally about the enclosure. Just then, an old drab colored duck waddled slowly from a nearby pond and passed between the proud peacock and the admiring crowd. The peacock became enraged and drove the duck back into the water. The beautiful bird suddenly became ugly with anger. The plain and awkward duck, having returned to the pond, was no longer unattractive. He swam and dove gracefully in the pond, unaware of the many eyes that now were not watching the peacock but were watching the duck. The people who had admired the peacock now loved the duck. What we need in

"Give Me That Old-Time Religion!"

our Independent, Fundamental, Bible-believing, Bible-preaching, premillennial, missionary-minded, soulwinning, temperamental, Baptist churches is about fifteen less peacocks and ten more ducks! Please, let me preach your funeral, "Mrs. Division."

III. Minister Discouragement

I Kings 19:4 says, *But he himself went a day's journey into the wilderness, and came and sat down under a juniper tree: and he requested for himself that he might die; and said, It is enough; now, O LORD, take away my life; for I am not better than my fathers.* This last person's funeral I would like to preach will be a shock. His name is "Minister Discouragement." In I Kings 19:4, the unknown prophet tells us about the significant lack of courage the prophet Elijah is showing under the shade of a juniper tree. It is almost hard to imagine that the lion of I Kings 18 is the kitty cat of I Kings 19. I might be able to handle it a little bit better if it were in I Kings that he was a lion and in II Kings that he was a kitty cat; but we are talking about his being a lion in Chapter 18, and a kitty cat in Chapter 19. He is whining, whimpering, sucking his spiritual thumb, and saying, "I just want to die." If he wanted to die, why did he not just slow down? Jezebel was hot on his heels, and she would have been more than happy to help him. He did not want to die. It was drama.

Mrs. Hamblin bought a shirt recently that she wears around the house. It says, "I don't do drama." I said, "Babe, get me about a hundred of those shirts, and I'll sell them at my book table. In fact, I'll just throw them at people that I think need it!" This is drama. He did not want to die. He is just exaggerating with the exasperation. He is discouraged, and it is this fatal spiritual disease that will take one from the highest of highs to the lowest of lows in the shortest span of time!

There was a medical doctor who made this statement, and I believe it is worth repeating. This medical doctor once said about this matter of discouragement, "Depression, gloom, pessimism, despair, discouragement: these slay ten human beings to every one murdered by typhoid, influenza, diabetes, or pneumonia." The tragedy about this person who is experiencing depression is that his name is on

Please, Let Me Preach Your Funeral

an ordination certificate. What is a tragedy about this person who is experiencing depression is not only that his name on an ordination certificate, but also that his name is right next to that title, Reverend. Friend, we need to know that a memorial service that a man of God would gladly volunteer to preach is the funeral of "Minister Discouragement."

The Bible says in Psalm 56:9, *When I cry unto thee, then shall mine enemies turn back: for this I know; for God is for me.* Newsflash: as long as the child of God knows God is in his corner, he will never ask Rabbi, Father, Reverend, or Elder Discouragement to sign the flyleaf of his Bible. It is "Minister Discouragement" who says to every young preacher that he comes in contact with, "I certainly wouldn't want to be like you starting my ministry in such a wicked day." Excuse me? This just in! Every day since the fall of man has been wicked. Just look at the history of America or the history of the world. Wickedness is at a faster pace and is more pronounced than it ever has been; but since we were kicked out of the Garden of Eden, it has been wicked big time. When "Minister Discouragement" talks about the blessings of Heaven in his life, it is always fifty years ago and never last week. He is of the mindset that revival, church growth, and doing great exploits for God will never happen.

I remember, as a young preacher, older preachers who would come along, and they would be "Minister Discouragement." They would say things like, "Man, you're going to be an evangelist? You'll never make it in evangelism. You've not been saved all that long. You've never pastored a church. You've never been to Bible College. You'll never make it in evangelism." Those same preachers have me in meetings, and it is amazing to hear them introduce me, as I am waiting to preach. They will say things like, "I've always been behind Dr. Hamblin. I always knew that he'd have a full calendar. I always knew that he'd be much in demand in evangelism." I am sitting there thinking to myself, "Liar, liar, pants on fire! Listen, Pinocchio, your nose is growing!" I just decided that if I ever got to be an older preacher, that I would do my best to encourage younger preachers. There are younger preachers all across America who have reaped the blessing of my being treated like trash as a younger preacher, because I decided and determined that I would

"Give Me That Old-Time Religion!"

encourage, strengthen, and try to be a blessing to them because I never got that when I started. It blows my mind now. I will preach for those guys, and they will act like they have always been there for me. The ones who would not even give me the time of day are now up in my face and ringing my cell phone off the hook. But in the early days, they never had time or concern. In fact, they never said anything that was encouraging. If they ever said anything, it was, "You're not going to make it. Who'd have you?" Oh, the brethren are just a blessing! It is this "Minister Discouragement" whose funeral I would love to preach.

I remember a few years ago, when my mentor Dr. Tom Malone, Sr. was still living. I received a phone call from him one afternoon. He said, "John, you're not going to believe it. I wasn't there, but I heard about it. We had a faculty member preach in chapel today that preached we can't have revival." That absolutely blows my mind! All through the Bible, we see that we can have revival, we can have a Spiritual awakening, we can have a mighty moving of God. I mean, the entire Bible is a manual on revival.

Dr. Malone said, "John, I'd never tell you what to preach. I would never do that, but can you give me two days back-to-back, as soon as you can, to come preach in chapel?" And again, he said, "I would never tell you what to preach, but if you might be able to preach on revival, that'd be a good thing."

I was more than happy to give him two days. Back-to-back I preached on revival: how we can have it, how we can experience it, and how God can still do it. Hallelujah! Friend, we can have revival. It is "Minister Discouragement" that has the mindset that we are not going to have church growth, and we are not going to have revival, and we cannot do great exploits for God. Please, please, please, let me preach your funeral, "Minister Discouragement."

Just off the wire! No pastor, evangelist, or missionary should ever counsel, preach, or even say "Hello" to people as long as he is getting his spiritual mail at Discouragement Avenue. They do not need counsel from someone who is discouraged. They do not need preaching from someone who is discouraged. They do not even need a hello or

Please, Let Me Preach Your Funeral

salutation from anyone who is discouraged. My discouragement could rub off on them. As a preacher, I am supposed to be setting the pace.

I read just a few days ago that the Devil decided to go out of business. It is just a parable, a fable, but I wish that he did. If the Devil went out of business, we would not have any bars, rock music, immorality, marijuana, or cocaine. Washington would be empty! But it is only a parable, a fable. It has been said that the Devil once decided to go out of business, and offered his tools for sale. They were attractively displayed. Trickery, hatred, jealousy, malice, deceit, sensuality, and many other evil tools, each marked with a sale price. But in the center was a wedge-shaped, much worn tool, priced higher than all the others.

"What is that?" Satan was asked,

"That is discouragement," he replied.

"But why is it so costly? Why is the tool of discouragement more costly than trickery, hatred, jealousy, malice, deceit, or sensuality? Why is it priced more?"

"Because it can do my evil work better than all the other tools. With it, I can make the lives of many folks to be of no value. I can make them just lie down, give up, and become useless, and they don't even know that I'm the one who uses it," said the Devil.

If this parable is true, and the Devil's favorite tool is discouragement, then I cannot help but wonder how much more powerful it is when that tool is standing behind a pulpit in the form of "Minister Discouragement." We have seen from the pages of the Bible, the memorial services that a man of God would gladly volunteer to preach. The memorial services that a preacher would say, "Please, please, let me preach your funeral. I know it is not appropriate. I know that Emily Post wouldn't like it. I know that it is not ethical for me to offer my services, but I am so glad that you are dead. May I preach your funeral?"

A man of God would love to preach the funeral of "Mr. Disbelief," "Mrs. Division," and "Minister Discouragement." By the way, if a preacher is ever called on to preach that funeral, I surely hope that he does not look into the casket and see me. I surely hope he does not look into the coffin and find my earthly tabernacle. The way we do not get in that

"Give Me That Old-Time Religion!"

casket is by using an old-fashioned altar and saying, "God forgive me for my disbelief. God, forgive me for my division. I may not be a preacher, but God, forgive me for my discouragement and how it affects other people." Please, let me preach your funeral!

Chapter Eight

What the Old-Time Religion Will Do for You

Jeremiah 6:16 says, *Thus saith the Lord, Stand ye in the ways, and see, and ask for the old paths, where is the good way, and walk therein, and ye shall find rest for your souls. But they said, We will not walk therein.* Notice the statement in this verse, *And ask for the old paths.* There is a vast difference between what the Old-Time Religion, which is salvation and the Lord Jesus Christ, and what the new age religion will accomplish for an individual. Their difference is as much as Heaven and Hell, as blessing and blistering, and as sulfur and splendor. In Jeremiah Chapter 6, we find the proclamation of God's sure judgment. Now, I would challenge people to go back to Jeremiah Chapter 6 and read carefully and prayerfully the thirty verses that make up this sixth chapter because it deals entirely and exclusively with the proclamation of God's sure judgment. The judgment wheel of God turns mighty slow; but yes, it turns mighty fine as well. This chapter can be easily outlined or laid out like this:

Verses 1-13 - The Watchman
Verses 14-15 - The Physician
Verses 16-17 - The Guide
Verses 18-30 - The Assayer

"Give Me That Old-Time Religion!"

It is while the prophet Jeremiah is dealing under the direct inspiration of the Holy Spirit with the guide that a person reads a self-evident scripture. Verse 16 says, *Thus saith the LORD, Stand ye in the ways, and see, and ask for the old paths, where is the good way, and walk therein, and ye shall find rest for your souls. But they said, We will not walk therein.* Never forget, if the old paths are the good way, then it will obviously produce a great work in a person's life. Now, I think it bears mentioning that in Jeremiah 6:16 we find the words, *the old paths.* Right in the back of the words, *the old paths*, are the words *where is the good way*. So, I believe an argument could be made, and we could make that argument very firm, that the old paths are the good way. If the old paths are the good way, then obviously it will produce a great work in any and every person's life who travels and traverses the old paths.

Friend, those of us who are unsaved and saved should be able to detect old-time evidence of an old-time encounter with God. There are three arresting things that the Old-Time Religion will do for an individual. I have experienced Old-Time Religion; and keep in mind, I am not talking about religion the way the world talks about religion. See, we do not offer religion; we offer a relationship with the Lord Jesus Christ. But when we talk about Old-Time Religion, Old-Time Christianity, and the Old-Time Way, there are some arresting things that the old-time salvation experience will do for a person whether that person is seven or seventy, male or a female, young or old.

I. It Will Put a Person in a Pew

Acts 3:1 says, *Now Peter and John went up together into the temple at the hour of prayer, being the ninth hour.* An arresting thing that the Old-Time Religion will do for an individual is that it will put him or her in a pew. In Acts Chapter 3, we find that Peter and John had gone to the temple at the hour of prayer. Now, in the temple, there were two times of prayer. There was prayer at 9:00 a.m. and then there was prayer at 3:00 p.m. The day for those believers was bookended by prayer. The physician Luke tells us that Peter and John are looking at their spiritual watches and see that it is time to pray. The Bible says that it was the ninth hour. So what do they do? They go to the temple. What do they

What the Old-Time Religion Will Do for You

do? They go to the place of worship. What do they do? They go to the church. That is what Old-Time Religion will do for us. It will put us in a pew.

Now, they did not go to church to get saved. They went to church because they were saved. I saw something that absolutely caused me to have my own personal camp meeting. As I was looking at Acts Chapter 3, I noticed that Peter and John are busy disciples. They are disciples who are being blessed and benefited in a meaningful way, but they had enough spiritual sense to know that they had better get to the church, get to the house of God, get to the temple. So what did they do? They went to church; and the Bible says that even though they were broke, they still went to church. That blessed my heart. In verse number 6, the Bible says, *Then Peter said, Silver and gold have I none...* They were Baptist preachers. They were broke! But what I like about that is that they did not take a job that would keep them out of church because they were broke! They did not have any money. They did not have any silver and gold, but still they went to the house of God. That is what Old-Time Religion will do. It will put us in a pew.

This kind of so-called Christian who could not be dragged to church with a team of wild stallions is a scriptural mutant. The Bible says in Psalm 122:1, *I was glad when they said unto me, Let us go into the house of the LORD.* David said, "When they just even talked about going to church, I was excited." David said, "When they just hinted about the possibility of going to church, I was glad." David got his King James Bible, got his family together, and then they headed to the house of God.

A pastor friend was telling me that in recent days his church had a great number of people saved. He had been telling me that in one week they had thirty saved, and over sixty saved during another week. It blesses my heart to see new converts who recently have been birthed from above, who recently have trusted Christ, and who are present for church. They are in the house of God enjoying the house of God. That is not new age salvation. That is old-time salvation. That is what salvation will do for us. It will put us in the pew. I am a little sick of the kind of salvation that never causes people to come to the house of God. They

"Give Me That Old-Time Religion!"

miss more services than they attend. Something is just not right with that scenario.

Thirty plus years ago, on a Sunday morning, the Word of God was preached, an invitation was given, I walked down the aisle, knelt at the altar, looked into an open Bible, and was birthed unto the family of God. Oh, when I got up from that altar, I was a different young man. In thirty plus years, there has not been a single Sunday or Wednesday night that I have missed other than sickness all this time. I was in church probably more than I am aware of, and I just want to go on record to say that that is exactly what Old-Time Religion will do for us. It will put us in a pew. I say this to the honor and glory and praise of Jesus: not one time has anybody had to make a call on me. Not one time has anybody ever had to promise me a Caribbean cruise to go to church. I still recall when I found out right after I got saved that I should come back on Sunday nights and Wednesday nights, and that we had this thing called visitation on Tuesday nights. I did not even know what it was, but I showed up for visitation because it was on the church schedule. I just thought that Christians are supposed to be in church. What a novel idea! I just knew that Christians were supposed to be faithful to the house of God. Old-Time Religion will put us in a pew.

II. It Will Put a Person on a Porch

Acts 20:20 says, *...but have shewed you, and have taught you publickly, and from house to house.* An arresting thing that the Old-Time Religion will do for an individual is that it will put him on a porch. The word *porch* means a platform before a dwelling. In Acts 20:20, the physician Luke tells us that the Apostle Paul is speaking to the elders and that he is giving them a charge. He is giving them clear instructions. Before he signs off, before they hug necks, before they go different ways, there was a real possibility, and it lay heavy upon the heart of those preachers and upon the heart of Paul, that there was a good chance that they would never meet again this side of Heaven. Paul is giving them a charge. But right in the midst of them, Paul says, "I have gone through Ephesus, and I have knocked on every door and talked to every person that I could. I tried to bring salvation to every person." I believe that with all of my heart and soul that that is exactly what Old-Time Religion will do for us. It will put us on a porch. This kind of salvation that never passes out a tract; this kind of salvation that never comes to an altar to pray for lost loved ones; this kind of salvation that never carries a burden for people who are busting Hell wide open is absolutely foreign to the Bible. We need a revival of Old-Time Religion, not new age religion. New age religion lets a person sign a card, put his name on the church roll, and never darken the doors of the house of God again. New age religion never sees a person pass out a Gospel tract nor makes a person feel like a heathen about it. Paul said, *I have taught you publickly, and from house to house.*

Let us quickly look at several places where the believer can witness. There is no such thing as a wrong place. Wherever there are saints and sinners, there is a situation for soulwinning. Some places where a believer can witness may shock us. The first place where the believer can witness is at the synagogue. Acts 14:1, *And it came to pass in Iconium, that they went both together into the synagogue of the Jews, and so spake, that a great multitude both of the Jews and also of the Greeks believed.* In Acts 14:1, Paul and Barnabas go into a religious den of the Devil, and they begin to witness and preach and tell people about Jesus. The result was that God blessed their effort and soulwinning. Someone may ask, "How can I do that? I can't walk into some place and say, 'Pardon me, I'd like to have a microphone.'" Usually at church they do not have open mic night. A person just cannot walk into a church service and say, "Excuse me, I have something to say that is a whole lot more important that what you're saying."

How in the world do we witness at a synagogue? Remember those experiences and occasions when a relative dies who is a member of what they thought was a "church"; but in light of the Bible, it is not a "church"? Out of respect for that loved one, we attend that service. Sitting in that service while whatever that goes on is going on, we get bored out of our minds because the Bible is not opened. The difference between a good church and a bad church is the Bible. While sitting there bored out of our minds, we realize that in our pocket or purse are Gospel tracts. In a sly, secretive way, we pull out 300 tracts and start filling those hymn

"Give Me That Old-Time Religion!"

books and the envelope racks with Gospel tracts. Only Heaven will tell when the very next Sunday, those people who came into that religious den of the Devil sitting there bored out of their minds like we were, killing time, open a hymn book and out comes a Gospel tract. They read it and the Spirit of God deals with their hearts, and right then and there, they get saved. They trust Christ. They are born again. We can witness at the synagogue!

The second place where believers can witness is at the store. Acts 17:17 says, *Therefore disputed he in the synagogue with the Jews, and with the devout persons, and in the market daily with them that met with him.* Someone may ask, "So, how do I witness at the store?" When we pay for our groceries, pull out a Gospel tract, and speak in a sweet, kind, and polite way. Say, "Ma'am or Sir, thank you for waiting on me. I want you to have a really good day, but I want even more for you to have a real good eternity. Let me give you something to read that's from the Bible. It won't take long to read because it's not like a Bible study." I have a problem with Gospel tracts for which one has to have a bookmark! If we will just give them a short, concise, Gospel tract, we will never know what the rest is but that they might take it to their break room or put in their pocket or Wal-Mart vest, pull it out later, read it, and be saved. We can witness as a believer at the store.

The third place where believers can witness is in the street. I love how practical the Bible is. Acts 5:42 says, *And daily in the temple, and in every house, they ceased not to teach and preach Jesus Christ.* We can go to somebody's house, knock on his door, and say, "I'm from the Open Door Baptist Church, and we are out looking to see if people have a church home. But more importantly, we're trying to find out if people are ready for eternity. If you were to die right now, do you know for sure that you would go to Heaven? Can I take the Bible and a few minutes of your time and introduce to you to the best friend I've ever had. His name is Jesus." Places where the believer can witness are the synagogue, the store, and in the street!

A couple of years ago, I was holding a revival meeting in Michigan. Before that revival meeting started, I had contracted pneumonia. I have had pneumonia five different times. I got a phone call from a young

What the Old-Time Religion Will Do for You

evangelist, and he said, "You know, I used to always hear you say that you take two weeks off a year." He said, "One week you say you take for your family, and the other week you save for pneumonia." So, I was preaching that revival meeting, and really, I should have been in the hospital. Truth be told, I should not have been preaching. The doctor said that I had one lung that was absolutely filled with fluid. So, I was like flying with one engine. A preacher needs his lungs to be able to preach. It helps to be able to breathe while preaching!

I started that revival meeting, sick as a dog, and the better part of wisdom would have been for me to be in the hospital, or at the very least, at home in bed. Our family doctor said, "All right, I will not put you in the hospital if you promise me that you'll only preach, and when you get done preaching, you'll go right home and get right in bed until you have to preach in the next service." I made him that agreement. Of course Mrs. Hamblin held me firmly to that. I started the revival meeting on Sunday morning, and I told the people, "I am sorry I'm not going to be able to fellowship with you like I want to. But after the service tonight, I'll stick around for a little bit. The doctor says, "I have pneumonia. I've got one lung filled with it, but I promise I'll stick around and fellowship a little bit." My driver and I had worked it out that just as soon as I get out of the pulpit, he would have the car running. It was in the dead of winter. I would get out as quickly as I could and get right home and in bed so that I would have some measure of strength to preach again that night. After I finished preaching, my driver had the car pulled to the curb. I took off the wet suit coat and put on a dry over coat and off we went. He was driving as quickly as he could. As we were traveling, we passed the Knights of Columbus. And God is my witness, Elvis Presley, walked into the Knights of Columbus. We both saw it at the same time. He looked at me and I said, "You know what, Elvis needs a tract. He spun around and pulled into the Knights of Columbus hall. I walked in, and of course there was security saying, "Excuse me, are you a member?" I said, "I'm a Baptist preacher, and I'm looking for Elvis!" I mean to tell you, they led me to where Elvis was. I said, "I am John Hamblin and God sent me by to give you this Gospel tract." I put that Gospel tract in

"Give Me That Old-Time Religion!"

his hand and Elvis said, "Thank you, thank you very much." Old-Time Religion will put us on a porch!

III. It Will Put a Person in a Pool

Acts 8:36 says, *And as they went on their way, they came unto a certain water: and the eunuch said, See, here is water; what doth hinder me to be baptized?* Last of all, an arresting thing that Old-Time Religion will do for a person is put him in a pool. In Acts 8:36, the physician Luke tells us of Phillip's witnessing to the Ethiopian eunuch. As I was reading it, I was just captivated. It is so amazing to see how the Ethiopian eunuch is reading the Bible and God sends Philip. Philip was an evangelist. Philip was in a big revival meeting and God said to him, "I want you to leave that revival meeting, and I want you to talk to an Ethiopian who's out in the desert." God is interested in one person just as much as He is interested in a multitude. There cannot be a multitude unless there is one person. One person makes a big difference.

> *God is interested in one person just as much as He is interested in a multitude.*

Philip leaves that revival meeting, and he goes down to the desert. It just so happens that there is this Ethiopian eunuch who is sitting on the back end of his chariot reading from Isaiah Chapter 53. Philip says, "Do you understand what you are reading?"

The eunuch says, "How can I understand except that some man should guide me?"

What happens next is that Philip takes that same portion of the Word of God and leads the eunuch to Christ. The eunuch gets saved. As they are traveling, they come upon a large body of water. The eunuch says, "Here's water. What doth hinder me to be baptized?"

That is what the Old-Time Religion will do for us. Every time, it will put us in a pool. What is so interesting about that statement is that Philip did not introduce the matter of baptism, the eunuch did. The eunuch introduced the matter of baptism after he was saved. The Bible does not teach baptism comes days later after conversion.

What the Old-Time Religion Will Do for You

The Bible does not teach that baptism comes weeks after conversion. The Bible does not teach that baptism comes years after the moment of conversion. The Bible does not teach months but minutes after a person is saved, he is to be baptized, immediately. We do not believe in infant baptism because the Bible does not teach it. We believe in instant baptism because the Bible teaches that.

I met a missionary a few months ago. He said, "Pray for my son." I am not being harsh in telling this because I think it illustrates the truth I want to drive home to each of our hearts. He said, "You need to pray for my son. We've been on the mission field for a number of years. My son's about twenty, twenty-one years of age. He's never been baptized." Now, Friends, that situation is an anomaly in the Bible. In the Bible, when people got saved, they got baptized. In the Bible, when people trusted Christ, they got baptized. This Ethiopian eunuch did not go through a ten week course on baptism. Did I say that Philip did not even mention baptism? It was the Ethiopian who mentioned baptism. Apparently the Ethiopian must have run across somebody who had Old-Time Religion. The Ethiopian must have known that when a person gets saved, he gets baptized! It is that identifying mark that we belong to the Master. When someone receives the truth about being born again, he will receive the truth about baptism. The Bible says in Acts 2:41, *Then they that gladly received his word were baptized...* They gladly got saved, and so they gladly got soaked!

A few years ago now, I was preaching in a revival meeting in Charlestown, Maryland. While we went in that revival meeting on Sunday morning, the pastor told me that there was a man in the audience who was lost. He said that the man's wife had said to the pastor that she felt that for the last couple of weeks, she was married to the Devil. He was unsaved and doing all those things that unsaved people do. The pastor said, "We have at least one man here who is lost." I said like I always do when I find out that there are lost people in the service. I said, "You know what? It would be a great day for them to get saved. It would be a wonderful service for them to trust Christ. This would be a wonderful service for them to get the Old-Time Religion. This would be a wonderful service for them to leave darkness and meet the Light of the

"Give Me That Old-Time Religion!"

World. This would be a wonderful service for that." So I preached that morning. I preached with a burden for that man that he might come to Christ. When the invitation was given, he was under heavy conviction. He hung on to the pew ahead of him until his knuckles were white; but thank God, the High Sheriff of Heaven was dealing with his heart. The Spirit of God was working him over; and finally, he let go of that pew. He left the world and met the Wonderful One. He left sin and met the Saviour. He left religion and got a relationship with Jesus Christ.

    He was back that Sunday night. He got saved Sunday morning and was back on Sunday night. I guess Old-Time Religion will put a person in the pew! He came back Monday and Tuesday nights. In fact, he sat on the second row right behind the preachers. He got a King James Bible. Nobody said anything about his hair; but on Tuesday, he walked into that revival meeting looking good. He had long hair, but since he got saved on Sunday morning, the Spirit of God moved into his heart, and now a great preacher – the Holy Spirit - lives in his body and he went to the barbershop. When we closed that revival meeting on Friday night, he came forward to be baptized. I knew that God was going to do something. I just knew that he was going to be baptized because that night he came with his whole family. He was absolutely eating it up. I could not preach too hard for him. It is amazing how salvation makes us like preaching! It is amazing. He was just days old in the Lord, and I could have taken the pulpit and threw it at him and landed it in his lap, and he would have just said, "Bring it on!" He brought his family with him that last night. He also had a grocery sack with him. I knew that in that grocery sack there would be a change of clothes. When the service was over, the pastor said, "Now we are going to baptize Tom, tonight. Tom got saved on Sunday morning, and Tom wants to be baptized." We sang some hymns while the preacher was getting ready. After about two or three songs, out came the preacher and Tom. Tom's little boy, five years of age was sitting right behind me. I will not soon forget it. He got out in the middle aisle of the church and was standing there, I mean right at attention. His eyes were glued on his father.

    The pastor said, "Tom, did you trust Christ as your Saviour"?

What the Old-Time Religion Will Do for You

Tom said, "Yes Sir, I have. Sunday morning I got saved." Man, the church shouted, and his wife wept. The members of his family were all standing with their eyes open wide.

The pastor continued, "Tom, upon the profession of your faith, I baptize you, my Brother, in the name of the Father, the Son, and the Holy Ghost. Buried in the likeness of His death..." As he began lowering him down, that little five-year-old boy clapped his hands and said, "Yeah, Daddy! Yeah, Daddy! Yeah, Daddy!"

I believe that is what the Old-Time Religion will do for us. It will put a person in a pool. And I believe that when a Christian follows the oracles of God in regard to baptism, when a Christian follows the commands of God in regard to baptism, I believe all Heaven says, "Yeah, believer! You've done the right thing! This is what the Old-Time Religion will do for you."

"Give Me That Old-Time Religion!"

Chapter Nine

And There Arose Another Generation after Them, Which Knew Not the Lord

Judges 2:6-10, *And when Joshua had let the people go, the children of Israel went every man unto his inheritance to possess the land. And the people served the LORD all the days of Joshua, and all the days of the elders that outlived Joshua, who had seen all the great works of the LORD, that he did for Israel. And Joshua the son of Nun, the servant of the LORD, died, being an hundred and ten years old.* I cannot read the eighth verse without making some type of a comment. This is the same Joshua that followed Moses.

Verses 9-10, *And they buried him in the border of his inheritance in Timnathheres, in the mount of Ephraim, on the north side of the hill Gaash. And also all that generation were gathered unto their fathers: and there arose another generation after them, which knew not the LORD, nor yet the works which he had done for Israel.* There is in this tenth verse a twelve word phrase that I wish to place a mental tent around—*and there arose another generation after them, which knew not the Lord.*

The apostasy of tomorrow's generation is the direct result of the apathy of today's generation. Unmistakable examples of this error are corrupt Bibles, shallow songs, and contemporary churches. When Bible truth does not move from the older generation to the younger generation, spiritual treason develops. *And there arose another generation after them which knew not the Lord.* In Judges Chapter 2, we find the introduction to the era of the judges. This chapter can be easily outlined or laid out like this:

>Verses 1-6 - The Missed Opportunity for Rededication
>Verses 7-10 - The Missed Opportunity for Training
>Verses 11-23 - The Missed Opportunity for Witness

It is while the prophet Samuel is dealing under the direct inspiration of the Holy Spirit with the missed opportunity for training that a person reads one of the most sobering, serious, and yes, staggering verses in all of the Scriptures: verse 10 says, *And also all that generation were gathered unto their fathers: and there arose another generation after them, which knew not the LORD, nor yet the works which he had done for Israel.* In Judges 2:10, we find death and decline. In the Hebrew language, the word *knew* means "for a certainty or comprehend." One well-known Bible student once wrote the following about our text: "The neglect of the fathers led to the apostasy of their sons."

The sister verse of Judges 2:10 is Exodus 5:2. There the Bible says, *And Pharaoh said, Who is the LORD, that I should obey his voice to let Israel go? I know not the LORD, neither will I let Israel go.* The generation after Joshua and the Pharaoh that held the children of Israel in bondage within the borders of Egypt had the exact same awareness of God. Someone may say, "Well, Pharaoh had no awareness of God." Absolutely, and neither did the generation after Joshua. When I saw this fact in my own personal study, my heart literally quaked. I thought about how that neither Pharaoh nor these people knew God. I would much rather stand before the judgment bar of God with Mother Theresa's profession of faith, than to stand before the judgment of God with their profession of faith.

Never forget that the generation behind us will have no perception of the preserved Bible, no comprehension of Christ, and no realization of real salvation if the generation before us does not guard and give truth to them. Do not miss that statement. It even bears repeating. There is another generation yet to come. The generation behind us will

> *Never forget that the generation behind us will have no perception of the preserved Bible, no comprehension of Christ, and no realization of real salvation if the generation before us does not guard and give truth to them.*

have no perception of the preserved Bible, no comprehension of Christ, and no realization of real salvation if the generation before us does not guard and give truth to them.

Sometimes we forget that someone else will sit in the pew in which we are sitting or will stand in the pulpit in which we stand. Many times, we are spiritually devastating and destroying another generation by our own sinful actions. We act like it is all about us. We act like we are the only ones that will sit where we sit and stand where we stand; but if Jesus stays His coming, there will be another generation. Consequently, the generation will be as lost as a softball in high weeds, unless we determine, decide, and desire to guard and give truth to them.

Now there are three serious iniquities that will bring ruination to the next generation. If selling out would only hurt us, that would be bad enough. If selling out only hurt us, it would be reason enough to preach against selling out. However my dear friend, it does not just hurt us. According to the written voice of God, it hurts others including the unseen generations. *And there arose another generation after them which knew not the Lord.*

I. Forgetting Former Preachers

Hebrews 13:7, *Remember them which have the rule over you, who have spoken unto you the word of God: whose faith follow, considering the end of their conversation.* A serious iniquity that will bring ruination to the next generation is forgetting former preachers. In Hebrews 13:7, the Apostle Paul tells us that we are to remember and revere those men of God who faithfully proclaimed and practiced the Word of God. The key word that unlocks the door of understanding of this verse for a person is that eight-letter word, *remember*. In the Greek language it means "to be mindful or to rehearse."

"Give Me That Old-Time Religion!"

Paul was not on some spiritual ego trip. This can be determined without any debate or discussion because he does not say, "Remember me;" but he does say, "Remember them." That is an all-inclusive phrase that covers every preacher's past, present, and future influencing and impacting the believer's life. In other words, the apostle of the church was saying, "Please, please, please do not let the mental grave of the memory and ministry of great men of God become unmarked and forgotten." Friend, we are spiritually devastating the next generation by forgetting former preachers such as Charles Haddon Spurgeon, G. Campbell Morgan, Dwight Lyman Moody, Reuben Archer Torrey, and T. DeWitt Talmage. The Bible says in Psalm 61:5, *For thou, O God, hast heard my vows: thou hast given me the heritage of those that fear thy name.*

In November of 2004, I was preaching a revival meeting at the Sixth Avenue Baptist Church. This church was started by a Baptist preacher named Robert Lowry. Robert Lowry wrote that great hymn of the faith that we often sing in our fundamental services, "Nothing but the Blood." Annie Hawks was saved at the Sixth Avenue Baptist Church. She also wrote a hymn that is in our hymnbook that we sing in our fundamental services, "I Need Thee Every Hour."

While I was preaching in Brooklyn, my intimate friend, Dr. Shelton Smith called me and said, "Now, John, I understand you're preaching in Brooklyn. I believe you'd find it interesting to visit the Greenwood Cemetery, the burial site of Ira Sanky, soloist and song leader for D. L. Moody."

Dr. Smith did not know it, but when I got to the Greenwood Cemetery, they have a kiosk. Not only is Sanky buried there, but Robert Lowry; J. C. Penney, the Christian businessman; and Samuel Morse, the inventor of the Morse code, who was a Christian as well. Henry Ward Beecher is another great man that is buried there. What Dr. Smith did not know until I shared with him after I had visited the Greenwood Cemetery, was that Talmage also pastored in Brooklyn. Talmage is probably my favorite preacher of the past to read. Talmage in every sense of the word was an orator. I entered Talmage's name into the kiosk and found where he was buried. Talmage's headstone is about the

And There Arose Another Generation

size of four baby grand pianos. When I visited Talmage's grave, before I even realized what I was doing, I stood there and with tears in my eyes, I saluted his headstone and said out loud, "Thank you, Dr. Talmage for the heritage and history that you've given to me. By the grace and help of God, I'll try to stay true to what you've given to me." When fundamental Christians fail to recall men of God like J. Wilbur Chapman, Billy Sunday, Bob Jones, Sr., R. G. Lee, Oliver B. Green, John R. Rice, Lester Roloff, Curtis Hutson, Jack Hyles, Tom Malone, and others, they soon will not realize their fundamental history. That is our heritage. That is our history. We have another generation that is coming. We will spiritually devastate and destroy that generation if we forget former preachers.

An easy way that this enormous problem can be effectively eliminated is by a church naming a Sunday school bus, a fellowship hall, a Sunday school room, or even a choir practice room after a great servant of God from yesteryear. I am Baptist-born and Baptist-bred, and when I die I will be Baptist-dead, but do not get hung up on a name. It is more than a name that makes a church a great church. At the height of Spurgeon's ministry, a person could not get a cab in London on the Lord's day without getting in that cab and having that cab driver say, "Are you going to Charlie's place?" They just assumed people were going to the Metropolitan Tabernacle to hear Spurgeon.

What would be wrong with taking a Sunday school bus and putting a picture of Spurgeon on the inside with a little biographical sketch and just calling it the Spurgeon bus? What about taking a Sunday school room and name it the Torrey Sunday school room? R. A. Torrey, was very articulate and very learned. R. A. Torrey was big on Bible study. He helped Mr. Moody start the Moody Bible Institute. After the home-going of D. L. Moody, he went to California and started another Bible institute, which is still in existence today. What about naming the fellowship hall, the Moody Hall? Homer Rodeheaver was the song leader and soloist of D. L. Moody. What about taking a choir practice room and naming it the Homer Rodeheaver Choir Practice Room? By doing those simple things, we are promoting and protecting and passing down our heritage and history to generations to come.

"Give Me That Old-Time Religion!"

In March of 1997, I had the wonderful experience of visiting Mount Hermon in Northfield, Massachusetts. This happens to be the birthplace, home, school, conference grounds, and burial plot of both D. L. Moody and his dear wife. If I were to make a list of the ten greatest experiences spiritually speaking of my existence, high on that list would be when I visited Mount Hermon.

The Moody Bible Institute was once a sacred learning institution, but now it is a secular learning institution. I stopped three students, and I told them who I was and that I was an evangelist and that D. L. Moody was one of my heroes. I asked those young men, "What can you tell me about Mr. Moody?" It was as if I shot all three of them. They dropped their heads and took what seemed like forever to answer. Finally, one of the three, as if he were going to turn the answer over, kicked the ground and looked up and said to me, "Sir, we really don't know much about this Moody fellow, but we think that maybe he's buried somewhere on this property." That is enough to make a stone weep.

I fear that the day will come in our fundamental churches when a preacher preaches on a Sunday morning and quotes Spurgeon or Rice that a church member will nudge another church member and say, "Who in the world is he talking about?" Forgetting former preachers will bring ruination to the next generation!

II. Falling Away from Fiery Preaching

Psalm 104:4 says, *Who maketh his angels spirits; his ministers a flaming fire.* A serious iniquity that will bring ruination to the next generation is falling away from fiery preaching. In Psalm 104:4, the unknown Psalmist tells us that it was God who fashions His angels into presences and His ministers into passionate preachers. The Bible snapshot of a preacher is not some cool clergyman sitting on a snack bar stool after the praise team has finished jumping and jiving, wearing a casual pair of pants and a turtleneck sweater and holding a tampered with Bible whom we cannot even hear when he is in the white heap of communicating past the second row of La-Z-Boy chairs.

Let me interject right here that Christian music should not make us wiggle. It should make us worship. God deliver us from this "Seven

And There Arose Another Generation

Eleven" music that has crept into our churches. "Seven Eleven" music is these choruses with seven words that we sing eleven times. There is not a better tune than, "Amazing grace! how sweet the sound, that saved a wretch like me! I once was lost, but now am found, was blind but now I see." or "At the cross, at the cross where I first saw the light, and the burden of my heart rolled away, it was there by faith I received my sight, and now I am happy all the day!" I also love, "Jesus paid it all, all to Him I owe; sin had left a crimson stain, He washed it white as snow." How about "Trusting Jesus" or "Pentecostal Power"? There is nothing that beats the hymns of the faith. They are called hymns because they are about Him! They are about Jesus, the Saviour, and the Redeemer of our soul. Therefore, we ought to call those mindless, unscriptural choruses "ITS" because they are not about Him.

I firmly believe that a preacher ought to look like a preacher. Politicians look like crooks. Mailmen look like mailmen. Grocery store cashiers look like grocery store cashiers. Plumbers look like plumbers. Mechanics look like mechanics. A preacher ought to look like a preacher.

I was in a meeting recently and one of these cool clergymen came sliding in with his collarless shirt. (He was wearing one of those stupid turtlenecks. I hate turtlenecks. It is like a weak man choking me.) He was one of those clergymen that will take some time out of his church calendar to have forty days of purpose. What he really needs is a forty-day revival meeting! When he came sliding in, I nudged another preacher, took out my money clip, and pulled out a twenty dollar bill. I slipped that $20 to that other preacher and said, "Why don't you go buy that idiot a shirt and tie because apparently, he doesn't have one." God deliver us from flip-flop, casual shorts, t-shirt, coffee cup kind of Christianity! Whatever happened to the old-time way? Whatever happened to just preaching? We are spiritually devastating the next generation by falling away from fiery preaching.

There are several sticks that will always build a fire in the pulpit. The scriptural pattern is Pentecost. Acts 2:3, *And there appeared unto them cloven tongues like as of fire, and it sat upon each of them.* The first stick that will always build a fire in the pulpit is enduement. If *cloven*

"Give Me That Old-Time Religion!"

tongues like as of fire could be seen upon the apostles of yesterday, then the convincing touch of God can be sensed upon the preachers of today. There is nothing that I pray for more than God's touch, breath, and power upon my preaching. I do not know how many times a day that I pray for it. Countless times I have put it on a sticky note, or on the flyleaf of my Bible that I might be reminded that what I need is that touch, that breath, that power from another world.

The second stick that will always build a fire in the pulpit with the scriptural pattern of Pentecost is excitement. Acts 2:14, *But Peter, standing up with the eleven, lifted up his voice.* There is something drastically wrong when a salesman gets more excited and more hot under the collar about his merchandise on the Home Shopping Network than a preacher does about his message on Wednesday night.

I will never forget as long as I live what my mentor, Dr. Tom Malone, Sr., said to me after I preached one night at the great Emmanuel Baptist Church. He said to me, "John, every time you preach, PREACH like you preached tonight." Dr. Smith, Dr. Malone, and I were in a Sword Conference a couple years ago. The night that Dr. Malone was not scheduled to preach, he and Mrs. Malone sat on the second row, left-hand side of the pulpit and prayed for Dr. Smith and I, and said, "Amen!" while we preached. When the service was over, we all went out to eat. Dr. and Mrs. Malone were sitting in the back seat of my car, Dr. Smith was in the passenger seat, and I was, of course, in the driver's seat. Dr. Malone leaned forward, and he squeezed my arm and squeezed Dr. Smith's arm and said, "John, you and Shelton stormed the fort tonight!" We need a revival of storming the fort! We need a revival of just raring back and preaching. Excitement is what we need!

The third stick that will always build a fire in the pulpit with the pattern of Pentecost is the Eternal Word of God. Acts 2:16, *But this is that which was spoken by the prophet Joel.* The day that it dawns upon a preacher's heart that it is not his word that he carries to the pulpit, but rather His Word, a new drive will come to his delivery.

Friend, we need to get back to just preaching—preaching by the letter and just letting it fly! I think that before every preacher preaches he ought to drink a big, tall glass of "I don't give a rip," and then "let it

And There Arose Another Generation

> *It is so refreshing to know that when we preach the Bible, we do not have to apologize, back up, halt, or hesitate. We can just open the Book and preach it!*

rip" with the Eternal Word of God. It is so refreshing to know that when we preach the Bible, we do not have to apologize, back up, halt, or hesitate. We can just open the Book and preach it! It is amazing how sometimes people get mad at the preaching. When we preach the truth, people are really not mad at the preacher. The preacher is just the newsboy. All we do when we preach is say, "Extra! Extra! Read all about it!" When we preach the Bible, we have backup. We can just preach it and know that God is going to bless it. When we preach the Bible, we do not have to worry about who likes it. If it is Bible, we do not have to backup, apologize, or wet our finger and see which way the wind of popularity is blowing.

I do not try to get people upset. That is not my agenda. My agenda is to preach the Bible. If I know I am going to preach the Bible and make somebody angry, I am going to preach the Bible. I have had people get up and storm out. It is not my goal to make people upset; but when I preach the Bible, sometimes folks get angry. Mrs. Hamblin was with me in a meeting recently, and I said, "Babe, if I get boring tonight, act like you're mad, because I preach better if someone's mad in the crowd." When I go back to the motel or to the house, and I pillow my head either on that motel pillow or very rarely on my own pillow, knowing that I did my best to preach this Book is a real comfort. Many can preach circles around me, but at least I know I did my best to stay true to the Word. It gives me sweet sleep.

The Eternal Word of God will build an excitement. It will build a fire. It is a stick from the pattern of Pentecost that will always work in building a fire in the pulpit. I wish that every person would realize the sticks that will always build that fire are enduement, excitement, and the Eternal Word of God.

Siberia is one of the most bone-chilling places on the planet. Average temperatures in Northeast Siberia range from below fifty degrees Fahrenheit in January to about sixty degrees Fahrenheit in

July. Now below Fahrenheit and above Fahrenheit is a great expanse. Because of its extremely harsh winters, the milkmen of that Russian region sometimes deliver their milk in chunks, not in quarts. One can imagine that the frozen solid milk is much easier for the seller to deliver; however, it is much harder for the buyer to digest. Let us make sure that every time we dispense the milk of the Word, it is not coming from our pulpits in frozen chunks.

III. Forsaking Fundamental Precepts

II Timothy 1:13 says, *Hold fast the form of sound words, which thou hast heard of me, in faith and love which is in Christ Jesus.* A serious iniquity that will bring ruination to the next generation is forsaking fundamental precepts. In II Timothy 1:13, the Apostle Paul tells us that we are to have a firm grip on the great tenants of the faith. It is not just that the Christian is to be loyal to the truth of God's Word, but they are to latch on to the very expressions in which that truth is conveyed. The word *fundamental* means "relating to a central structure or facts." The word *precepts* means "a command or a principle." A person must understand that the fundamental precepts are the verbal inspiration and the very preservation of the Bible.

When a preacher preaches and he says, "I believe in the verbal inspiration of the Bible," he is not going to get an *amen* from me quite yet. I am glad he believes in the verbal inspiration; however, when he takes that next step and says that he believes in the very preservation, then he will get an *amen* from me.

Either the Bible is inspired and preserved or the Bible is neither inspired nor preserved. We cannot have one without the other. The same God that takes care of inspiration is the God that takes care of preservation. Therefore, if one's pastor frequently hollers about the Bible, holler, "Amen!" Rejoice when he preaches this way because it is a fundamental precept.

What about the virgin birth? People may say, "The virgin birth is not a big deal." Read the Bible! The virgin birth does matter!

I read recently where Billy Sunday was in a cooperative meeting. There were preachers in that meeting from a number of churches.

And There Arose Another Generation

Someone had approached Billy Sunday as he came into the service that night and said, "Mr. Sunday, I hate to tell you; but there's a preacher on the platform, a cooperating church, that does not believe in the virgin birth." From what I have read of Mr. Sunday, he was somewhat shy out of the pulpit, and a lion in the pulpit. When they said that to him, it was as if he did not even hear it. It was as if he did not really comprehend what was said. He slightly nodded his head, and they progressed with the service. Homer Rodeheaver lead the singing and did some specials. Billy Sunday took the offering, and then it came time for preaching. Billy Sunday got up and said, "Now folks we're glad that you're here, and we're happy that you're in the tabernacle, but you'll pardon my back." He turned the pulpit around to face the cooperating preachers that were sitting on the platform. Billy Sunday preached a blistering sermon on the virgin birth to those preachers and said something along the lines, "I understand that there is some scallywag on this stage that doesn't believe that Jesus was virgin born. You'll fry in Hell if you don't repent and get saved!"

The virgin birth and the vicarious death are fundamental precepts. We should be glad we do not have to go to Hollywood to find out about Jesus' death. We just go to the Book. The Book is always better than the movie! I would never have imagined that the day would come when Baptists would take their church to the movies! If they are going to the movies, they will be going to the dance hall next. They might as well. They are already doing it on the platform. A person does not have to go to Hollywood to find out about the Bible. He just has to blow the dust off his Bible and read it.

The victorious resurrection is a fundamental precept. The song writer told it like this: "Up, from the grave He arose; with a mighty triumph o'er His foes; He arose a victor from the dark domain, and He lives forever with His saints to reign. He arose! He arose! Hallelujah! Christ arose!" That is the victorious resurrection. That is fundamental.

The visible return of the Saviour is also a fundamental precept. It is not just about us; it is also about the next generation. We are spiritually devastating that generation by forsaking fundamental precepts. In Acts Chapter 2, we find what I call a golden nugget of truth from the

"Give Me That Old-Time Religion!"

goldmine of the Bible. Acts 2:42 says, *And they continued stedfastly in the apostles' doctrine and fellowship, and in breaking of bread, and in prayers.* This is right where we live. This is right where we find ourselves today. Notice that God does not put fellowship in front of doctrine. The Ecumenicalist and the Charismatics do that, but God puts doctrine first, then fellowship. The reason we have so many spiritual Benedict Arnolds today is that they have spiritual dyslexia. They switch the words *doctrine* and *fellowship*. They say, "We just need to get together." Their statement of faith is to get together and believe nothing. We cannot have fellowship unless we have doctrine. When we have doctrine, then we have fellowship. Fellowship before doctrine equals compromising the truth. Doctrine before fellowship equals contending for the truth. There is a vast difference.

There is a man by the name of Donald Tracey. Donald Tracey's son, Scott, worked one summer on the S. S. Edwin H. Gotts, a one thousand-foot ore carrier. Donald told me that the captain allowed Scott to steer the great ship several times. One day when Scott was in the wheel house, the navigator said to him, "Now Scott, we're going to come to a marker and you're going to need to find that marker. I will help you, but you're going to need to find that marker. You will take the binoculars and will read the number off of the marker, and then together, we will look at the chart. When we find that marker on the chart, we will be told to look at the shore and find a white house with red trim. When we find the marker, read the number off the marker, and match it with the chart, look out of the wheel house, find that white house with red trim, and then we'll turn so many degrees, and we'll make the bend." So Scott, steering the S. S. Edwin H. Gotts came upon the marker and matched it with the charts. He then began to look out of the wheel house to the shore, to look for the white house with red trim. He looked endlessly and never found it. Suddenly, the captain burst into the wheel room and said, "Why is it that you've not turned the ship? We should have been making the turn by now. If you don't turn soon, we'll run aground." The captain looked at the chart and found the buoy that Scott and the navigator had found. He matched the number on the marker on the buoy to the chart. He looked out of the wheel house and tried to find the white house with red trim, but he could not find it either. Suddenly, almost at the very literal last second, it dawned on him that someone had painted the house. Now it was yellow and green. The white house with red trim was now a yellow house with green trim. Literally, at the last second they turned the ship.

If we do not make the Bible a big deal in the auditorium, then we will have the NIV in the Sunday school room. Preachers who say that the Bible is not going to be a big deal in their church, Christians who leave a fundamental church to go to a contemporary church, and preachers who take bus loads of their people to Billy and Franklin Graham Crusades are taking placating paints and are changing God's sign posts from white and red to yellow and green. If that were not bad enough, the ship of another generation is heading for the rocks.

And there arose another generation after them, which knew not the LORD. What a phrase! What an expression! What a statement! It is not all about us; it is about a generation that is yet unseen, and yet to come behind us!

"Give Me That Old-Time Religion!"

Chapter Ten

The Most Important Piece of Furniture in the Church

Nehemiah 8:1-4 reads, *And all the people gathered themselves together as one man into the street that was before the water gate; and they spake unto Ezra the scribe to bring the book of the law of Moses, which the LORD had commanded to Israel. And Ezra the priest brought the law before the congregation both of men and women, and all that could hear with understanding, upon the first day of the seventh month. And he read therein before the street that was before the water gate from the morning until midday, before the men and the women, and those that could understand; and the ears of all the people were attentive unto the book of the law. And Ezra the scribe stood upon a pulpit of wood, which they had made for the purpose...*

If a person were to pose the question to a group of fundamental parishioners, "What is the single most prominent piece of furniture in the house of God?" The answers would range from the predictable to the pathetic. Some would say the piano or the organ. (By the way, those are not furniture; they are instruments.) Others would answer the chairs in the choir. Those who seem to have a superior, spiritual spirit would say the Lord's Supper Table. However, all of those answers would be wrong. The weightiest piece of furniture in the house of God is the one where the eternal Word of God is faithfully and fervently declared. In

"Give Me That Old-Time Religion!"

the book of Nehemiah Chapter 8, we find a great Bible conference led by the priest and scribe Ezra. This chapter can be easily outlined or laid out like this:

Verses 1-6 - The Communication
Verses 7-8 - The Clarification
Verses 9-12 - The Celebration
Verses 13-18 - The Continuation

And Ezra the scribe stood upon a pulpit of wood, which they had made for the purpose... Ezra 8:4 is the first time, and for that matter, the only time the word *pulpit* is ever used in the entire Bible. That would make the mentioned pulpit the oldest pulpit in the history of mankind.

The word *pulpit* in the Hebrew language means "a tower of wood." The theme of this entire chapter is "The Book." Never forget in the annals of earth and eternity, that it is the sacred desk that thunders the Book which is the very center of everything that God has done or is about to do in a nation, a home, or in a soul of a man. Do not miss that. It even bears repeating. In the annals of earth and eternity, it is the sacred desk that thunders the Book which is the very center of everything that God has done or is about to do in a nation, a home, or in the soul of a man. What the saved and the unsaved must understand is that the most important piece of furniture in the house of God is the pulpit.

There are three things a fundamental pulpit represents that make it paramount furniture. Now again, it is not the organ, the piano, the chairs on the platform, or even the Lord's Supper table. The most important piece of furniture in a fundamental church is a fundamental pulpit. With the Lord's help I would like to look at the pulpit differently than it has ever been looked at before. There are three things that a fundamental pulpit represents that make it the most important, paramount, and inspired piece of furniture in the house of God.

I. The Pulpit Stands for Salvation.

I Corinthians 15:1-2 says, *Moreover, brethren, I declare unto you the gospel which I preached unto you, which also ye have received,*

The Most Important Piece of Furniture in the Church

and wherein ye stand; By which also ye are saved, if ye keep in memory what I preached unto you, unless ye have believed in vain. A reason why the fundamental pulpit is the most important piece of furniture in the house of God is that it represents salvation. In I Corinthians 15:1-2, the Apostle Paul tells us that he proclaimed the Gospel to the Corinthian believers resulting in their being placed in the family of God. Not only did he remind them of the truth that saves them, but he also rebuked those who attempted to tamper with the truth of the bodily resurrection. Paul was not one bit bashful about declaring to the Corinthians the cross, the corpse, and the conquered tomb of the Lord Jesus Christ. Paul was not afraid to announce to the Corinthian Christians all those charlatans who would undermine their faith in the conquered tomb. However, an individual must keep in the forefront of his mind that all this revolved around that eight-letter word *preached*.

Mrs. A. Katherine Hanky must have had the apostle of the church upon her heart when she picked up the hymn writer's pen and started to write those heart-penetrating words:

> I love to tell the story,
> For those who know it best
> Seem hungering and thirsting
> To hear it like the rest.
> And when, in scenes of Glory,
> I sing the new, new song,
> 'Twill be the old, old story
> That I have loved so long.
>
> I love to tell the story,
> 'Twill be my theme in Glory,
> To tell the old, old story
> Of Jesus and His love.

Friend, we must understand that the reason the fundamental pulpit is the most important piece of furniture in the house of God is because it represents salvation. The Bible says in I Corinthians 1:21,

"Give Me That Old-Time Religion!"

For after that in the wisdom of God the world by wisdom knew not God, it pleased God by the foolishness of preaching to save them that believe. Mark it down. Lost souls do not stand much of a chance of being saved and churches are speeding toward modernism when wheels are put on a pulpit. There is not one place we can find in the written voice of God where God smiles when the pulpit is permanently pushed off the platform for praise teams, productions, praise bands, power lifting, promotions, and other religious poppycock. It is not in the Book.

Without question, the most soul-moving illustration that I personally know of a person being saved as a result of preaching would have to be an eighteen-year-old man by the name of John. One Sunday morning, this young man walked in the auditorium of the Ambassador Baptist Church in Allen Park, Michigan. After a heart-lifting song service, the preacher mounted the pulpit, read his text of Acts 16:30, and then announced the subject of his sermon, "What Must I Do to be Saved?" At the close of that forty-five minute, spirit-filled, red-hot message, he started the invitation. Just as that church organist and pianist began playing "Just as I Am," the young man, now under heavy Holy Spirit conviction, came forward. He knelt at the altar, looked into an open Bible, and at 12:20 p.m. was birthed into the family of God. John was baptized immediately. (By the way, the Bible does not teach infant baptism but rather instant Baptism.)

Two weeks later, he surrendered to preach. Within thirty days of being saved, he began to preach; and at this very moment is somewhere preaching. While holding a fall revival meeting on his actual twenty-fifth anniversary of being saved and in the ministry, a dear preacher friend of his got the same pulpit that the preacher preached from when John was saved which happened to be the first pulpit from where John preached. This preacher placed it on the platform for John to use in that revival meeting.

Again, I would have to say without question that it would have to be the most soul-moving illustration that I know in regards to preaching and putting someone in the family of God. By the way, I think I forgot to give John's last name. It is Hamblin. The pulpit is the most important piece of furniture in the church because it stands for salvation.

II. The Pulpit Stands for Separation.

Psalm 40:9 says, *I have preached righteousness in the great congregation: lo, I have not refrained my lips, O LORD, thou knowest.* A second reason why a fundamental pulpit is the most important piece of furniture in the house of God is that it represents separation. In Psalm 40:9, the psalmist David tells us in a messianic psalm that during the Lord Jesus Christ's earthly ministry, He would proclaim the truth to great crowds without pulling any punches. Some people think that Jesus was a great teacher, and He was. Not only was He a teacher, but Jesus was also a preacher.

In Psalm 40:9, the Bible says that Jesus would preach to the great congregation; and His preaching would deal with righteousness. This was clearly and convincingly fulfilled in Luke 4:16. The word *righteousness* basically means "right living." People cannot live right until they first leave wrong. Friend, we must understand that the reason why a fundamental pulpit is the most important piece of furniture in the house of God is that it represents separation.

Now there are several things that the Biblical doctrine of separation sets out to straighten. First of all, separation sets out to straighten conduct. Romans 12:2 says, *And be not conformed to this world: but be ye transformed by the renewing of your mind, that ye may prove what is that good, and acceptable, and perfect, will of God.* Separation for a believer will never affect his behavior until it first affects his brain.

> *Separation for a believer will never affect his behavior until it first affects his brain.*

Separation does not start with a hem; it starts with the head. When it starts with the head, it will always reach the hem.

A second thing that the Biblical doctrine of separation sets out to straighten is clothes. I Timothy 2:9-10 says, *In like manner also, that women adorn themselves in modest apparel, with shamefacedness and sobriety; not with braided hair, or gold, or pearls, or costly array; But (which becometh women professing godliness) with good works.* Modest

"Give Me That Old-Time Religion!"

apparel is basically dressing Monday through Saturday the way right-with-God Christians dress on Sunday.

A third thing that the Biblical doctrine of separation sets out to straighten is company. II Corinthians 6:17 says, *Wherefore come out from among them, and be ye separate, saith the Lord.* No Christian who hangs out with bartenders, blasphemers, or Bible correctors is going to walk closely with God for a considerable length of time. A person can tell me whom he keeps company with, and I can tell him what his spiritual future will be a month from now. If we want to be right with God a month from now, then we need to run with those who are right with God now. Every person needs to realize that the things the doctrine of Biblical separation always sets to straighten out are conduct, clothes, and company.

I read about a sailor many years ago who had returned from a whaling voyage. Upon his return, he had heard an eloquent preacher. When asked how he liked the sermon, the sailor replied after the service, "It was ship-shape. The mast was just high enough. The sails and rigging all right, but I did not see any harpoons." When a vessel goes on a whaling voyage the main thing is to get whales. Whales do not come because one has a fine ship. One must go after the whales and harpoon them. The old sea dog paused for a long time, then concluded, "I think the preacher must be a whaler." When from the pulpit a Christian is hit with a harpoon that is labeled separation, he should not think about moving his membership. He should consider making a motion at the next business meeting that the preacher receives a raise in his salary. The pulpit stands for separation.

III. The Pulpit Stands for Supernatural Power.

I Corinthians 2:4 says, *And my speech and my preaching was not with enticing words of man's wisdom, but in demonstration of the Spirit and of power.* The last reason why the fundamental pulpit is the most important piece of furniture in the house of God is that it represents supernatural power. In I Corinthians 2:4, the Apostle Paul tells us that every time believers in the church of Corinth heard him preach, they did not hear an eloquent speaker, but rather an energized preacher.

The Most Important Piece of Furniture in the Church

When one listens closely and carefully to the apostle of the church, they discover the vast difference between public speaking and speaking from the pulpit. On a personal note, I call that preaching far outside one's ability with the breeze of Heaven upon it.

Charles Hadden Spurgeon once said, "You might as well expect to raise the dead by whispering in their ears as you hope to save souls by preaching to them if it were not for the agency of the Spirit." Friend, we must understand that the reason why a fundamental pulpit is the most important piece of furniture in the house of God is that it represents supernatural power. The Bible says in Psalm 62:11, *God hath spoken once; twice have I heard this; that power belongeth unto God.*

Any preacher's education, experience, eloquence, and even excitement is as worthless as last year's birthday balloons unless it is enveloped with the power of God. I am not against education. If a person does not have an education, he ought to get an education. However, education will not take the place of enduement.

I am not against experience. I think that the longer one preaches, the more experiences he will have. He then will be able to draw from the well of experience. Nonetheless, the well of experience cannot take the place of the well of enduement.

I am not against eloquence. I realize that words are my tools just as the saw is the tool of the carpenter, or as the plunger is the tool of a plumber, or as the wrench is the tool of a mechanic. I realize, that as a preacher, words are my tools. I strive to be clear, concise, convicting, and convincing; however, eloquence cannot take the place of enduement. I am not against excitement. I am for enthusiasm and excitement. It was Uncle Bud Roberson that said, "The reason that there are icebergs in the pews is because there are polar bears in the pulpit." I can think of a number of preachers who I believe need a transfusion, and what they need in that transfusion is for the blood to be taken out and enthusiasm to be pumped back in. Enthusiasm and excitement cannot take the place of an enduement of the Spirit of God. That is why the words of the almost forgotten hymn should ring in the soul of the preacher as he steps into the sacred desk:

"Give Me That Old-Time Religion!"

Brethren, we have met to worship
And adore the Lord our God;
Will you pray with all your power,
While we try to preach the Word?
All is vain unless the Spirit
Of the Holy One comes down;
Brethren, pray, and holy manna
Will be showered all around.

During the funeral of evangelist Billy Sunday, a strange incident occurred when the people came to view his body. A printer who looked into the casket was deeply moved in a spiritual way. While he gazed into the face of the evangelist who now lay in stillness of death, the printer made a consecration to God. Three times he made this dedication: once as he peered into the casket, again as he left the church (the same Moody Memorial church that holds 4,400), and again when he reached his car. His dedication was this: "Lord, make me a soulwinner."

The very next day, a man came into his print shop, handed him a tract and said, "Would you print this tract for me?" The printer's answer was a definite, "Yes." From that moment on, he began to print tracts for the Gospel work and continued to do so for many years. What a moving incident!

One could trace that back to a known practice of Mr. Sunday when he preached. For every time he stood in the pulpit, he placed his sermon notes on the top of his open Bible. The spot where his notes would be laid was Isaiah 61:1. They tell me that in Mr. Sunday's Bible, the page that would wear out first would be Isaiah 61. When he would get up to preach, he would mount up the pulpit, open his Bible, and lay his notes upon the verse that says, *The Spirit of the Lord God is upon me; because the LORD hath anointed me to preach good tidings unto the meek; he hath sent me to bind up the brokenhearted, to proclaim liberty to the captives, and the opening of the prison to them that are bound.* It is amazing that a promise for the power of God in preaching was fulfilled in the casket of evangelist Billy Sunday!

The Most Important Piece of Furniture in the Church

The most important piece of furniture is not an organ, a piano, a music class, the chairs, the choir or even the Lord's Supper table. The pulpit is the most important piece of furniture in the church. Although we will forever look differently upon the pulpit, it is not only the most important piece of furniture in the house of God, but it is also the most important piece of furniture in an unbeliever and a believer's life. The pulpit is where we hear the truth, the Gospel, and the words, "This is what you ought to do. This is what you ought not to do." It is the place of hope, help, healing, and sometimes some hard truths. Therefore, the pulpit is the most important piece of furniture in the church!

"Give Me That Old-Time Religion!"

Chapter Eleven

When Senselessness Gets Sensible

Luke 15:17 says, *And when he came to himself, he said, How many hired servants of my father's have bread enough and to spare, and I perish with hunger!* In this verse, there is a six-word statement that I wish people to place a mental tent around. It is the six-word statement, *And when he came to himself.* As hard as it is to believe and as strange as it may sound, stupid can get a wake-up call and within a few short seconds become smart. In Luke Chapter 15, we find the Lord Jesus Christ speaking of lost treasure. Now, I would challenge people to go back to Luke Chapter 15 and read carefully and prayerfully the thirty-two verses that make up this chapter, underlining and underscoring every time that they find the word *lost*. The word *lost* is the theme, thrust, and topic of this chapter. The Lord Jesus Christ deals with lost treasures. This chapter can be easily outlined or laid out like this:

    Verses 1-7 - The Lost Sheep
    Verses 8-10 - The Lost Shekel
    Verses 11-32 - The Lost Son

It is while the physician Luke is dealing under the direct inspiration of the Holy Spirit with the lost son, that a person witnesses

"Give Me That Old-Time Religion!"

Mr. Idiot take off a dunce cap and Dr. Intelligent put on a cap and gown. *And when he came to himself...* This same expression is used to describe the sleep-walking Peter when he was delivered from prison. In Acts 12:11, the Bible tells us how that the same expression, the same wording, the same phrase is used. There the Bible says, *And when Peter was come to himself, he said, Now I know of a surety, that the Lord hath sent his angel, and hath delivered me out of the hand of Herod, and from all the expectation of the people of the Jews.*

Friend, those of us that are saved need to come to ourselves in the hog pen so that we can quickly make it back to the home place. Now, no one will ever come back to the will, way, and work of God until, like that prodigal, he comes to himself. Let us notice when senselessness gets sensible. From Luke, Chapter 15, there are three things that always happen when the foolish Christian becomes the wise Christian. One may want to take a pencil and somewhere in his Bible, scratch these things down; but my, how much better it would be if God would take an eternal pen and write these things upon all of our hearts.

I. When You Remember the Father Has a Provision

Verse 17 says, *How many hired servants of my father's have bread enough and to spare, and I perish with hunger!* The foolish Christian becomes the wise Christian when he remembers that the Father has a provision. In Verse 17, the prodigal says to himself that back home the father's servants have it better than he does; the father's laborers have it better than he does; the father's workers have it better than he does. Here he is in a pigsty, and it dawns on him that back home the father's servants have it better than he has it. If just the hired servants push away from the table before all the platters and plates are empty, just imagine what the son's and daughter's table looks like!

I love that story in I Kings 17 where Elijah is at the Brook Cherith. God has a place for us. We are either in the will of God or we are out of the will of God. God has a station, a set place for us in the will of God. I think of my mentor, Dr. Tom Malone, Sr.; God bless his sainted memory. He used to say, "You can be in the will of God geographically and be out of the will of God spiritually." So, we should be in the will of God not

When Senselessness Gets Sensible

only geographically, but also spiritually. Here, we find Elijah from that account of I Kings 17 at the Brook Cherith. Again, God has a will for us. The will for me is to be an evangelist and to crisscross this country trying to nudge a prodigal nation back to God. What I am trying to say is God has a will for each of us. The will of God for the Prophet Elijah was to be at the Brook Cherith. Here, he is on the backside of nowhere; but it is the will of God for him. It is right where God wants him to be.

Now, there is something that happens there, something that transpires. It absolutely thrills my heart. The Bible says, in I Kings 17:6, *And the ravens brought him bread and flesh in the morning, and bread and flesh in the evening; and he drank of the brook.* Here he is in the will of God. He has bread and flesh in the morning and in the evening. As he is in the will of God, God sends ravens to feed him. I have heard about meals on wheels, but these are meals on wings as God is taking care of someone who is not just His prophet, but His child. I have come to this pulpit to say loud and clear and in an unmistakable way that a person cannot starve in the will of God. He cannot get skinny in the will of God. He cannot go without sustenance in the will of God. Listen, when senselessness gets sensible, when stupid gets smart, when dumb gets a degree, all of a sudden, we will realize that at the father's house, back in the will of God, there is provision.

Every morning, the ravens come. What do the ravens bring to Elijah? They bring to him bagels and bacon! And every evening, the ravens come. What do they bring? They are not bringing cubed steak or Spam. They are not even bringing sardines. They are carrying red-skinned potatoes and filet mignon wrapped in bacon. Elijah is getting fat and living high on the hog as he is in the will of God. There is no better place in all the world for a Christian to be than right smack dab in the middle of the will of God.

> *There is no better place in all the world for a Christian to be than right smack dab in the middle of the will of God.*

In recent days, we have let the news media get us all worked up, frazzled, and worried because of what they are calling a financial crash. Now, if this is a financial crash or a

"Give Me That Old-Time Religion!"

financial crunch, my question is why is it that all the restaurants I eat in are full? If this is a financial crash and a financial crunch, then why is it that all airplanes that I climb on are full? If there is a financial crunch or a financial crash, then how come all the malls that I pass are full? I am afraid that we have some Christians that are buying into this scare tactic that the world is coming to an end. We have some Christians who have this "Chicken Little" syndrome, thinking the sky is falling. I am here to say that if gas gets up to ten dollars per gallon, I am still holding my revival meetings. If the whole bottom falls out of this thing, I am still going to stay true to God. By His grace and with His help, I am still going to tithe. I am still going to trust Him. I am still going to give offerings. Let us not buy in to this idea that the end of the world is coming. I do not care what the price of gold is. I do not care what happens in Wall Street. I do not care how much gasoline may cost. There is a God in Heaven Who has promised to take care of us. It happens when senselessness gets sensible.

    I have a dear preacher friend whose car engine blew up. It would cost $2,800 to get it fixed. This preacher friend of mine could have told the church that he pastors, "I've got a need" and before he even put a period on that statement that church would have met the need, but that is not how he did it. Instead, he did this novel thing called pray. Instead of telling everybody about it, instead of telling his friends about it, instead of telling the church that he pastored about it, he just told Jesus about it. He preached on a Sunday morning, and while he was preaching, he was somewhat animated. The problem with our preaching today is that it is not authoritative, anointed, or animated! God deliver us from this kind of preaching that is nothing more than a glorified book report. If a man does not scream when he preaches, he should just sit down and let somebody else get up and scream since he will not.

    While he was preaching, he took off his suit coat and laid it over a chair on the platform and kept preaching. When the service was over, he drove his bus and took all the kids home, met his family at a restaurant for dinner, and then remembered that his suit coat was back on the platform. He thought, "I'll get it tonight. I won't have any need for it this afternoon." When he got back to the church, during the song service he went to the platform to get his coat that he had placed on his chair. While the song leader was leading the singing, before he would be there to moderate, he slipped on his coat. As he put his coat on, he felt something in the inside pocket, something that he did not remember being there during the morning service. So reaching into the inside pocket, he pulled out a large envelope. The envelope said, "From your guardian angel." The curiosity was too much. While the song leader was leading the singing, he popped open the envelope and looked inside. There was a cashier's check for $2,800! When we are in the will of God, God will take care of us. God knows our address. God knows our cell phone number. God knows our social security figures. Because God knows where we are, God can send exactly what we need where we are. When senselessness gets sensible, we will remember that the Father has a provision!

II. The Father Has a Pardon

Please look at verse 18. *I will arise and go to my father, and will say unto him, Father, I have sinned against heaven, and before thee.* When the foolish Christian becomes wise, he will recall that the Father has a pardon. In verse 18, the prodigal is rehearsing what he is going to report to the father. He wants every word to be perfect. He wants every pause to be in its place. He wants there to be an obvious pathos to his report and more importantly, to his repentance. What I love about verse 18 is that he is making no excuse. I am sick and tired of people who get caught doing wrong and want to say it is someone else's fault. I am a bit tired of hearing them say, "Well, it's because of my environment. It's because I didn't get a tricycle when I was two. It is because I never had a puppy or a cat." The reason why we are what we are is that we are wicked, low-down sinners. We need to quit making excuses and realize that we are what we are because of sin. I appreciate the prodigal for not making an excuse, for not coming up with some lame reason for the depravity and debauchery of his own depraved heart. It says in verse 18, *I have sinned*, not a mistake, or a misstep, He said, *I have sinned*. When the foolish Christian becomes the wise Christian, he recalls that the Father has a pardon.

"Give Me That Old-Time Religion!"

Now, there are several truths that picture the fullness of God's forgiveness for all prodigals. One Bible commentary called this the school in the pigsty. There are some lessons being learned here, life-changing lessons, and several truths that picture the fullness of God's forgiveness for all prodigals. That thrills my heart, because it is not just some prodigals or certain prodigals, but it is all prodigals. First of all, a truth that pictures the fullness of God's forgiveness for all prodigals is that the father is looking. Luke 15:20 says, *And he arose,* (that is the prodigal) *and came to his father. But when he,* (the prodigal) *was yet a great way off, his father saw him.* This verse seems to indicate before the son saw the father, the father saw the son. Before we ever get to an altar to get right with God, Jesus sees us. When the thought of how to get right with God percolates in our cranium God pays attention to it. I believe every time that we have a church service on Sunday morning, Sunday night, mid-week prayer meeting, tent meeting, revival meeting, or missions conference, that the eyes of God are upon the altar looking for people who will get right with Him. God is looking for people who will say, "God, I'm wrong, and You're right. God, I made a mess of this thing. I need Your mercy in a great magnitude." God is looking!

A second truth that pictures the fullness of God's forgiveness is the father's longing. Verse 20, *...and had compassion, and ran...* The two are inseparable. When one has compassion, it leads him to action. If I say that I have compassion and it does not lead me to action, then my compassion is suspect. If I say that I have compassion upon a lost and dying world and never pass out Gospel tracts, if I say that I have a burden for lost souls and I never go to the altar to pray for them, if I say that I want to see my family, friends, and fellow workers won to Christ and I do not have any testimony that God could use to bring them to Christ, then my compassion is suspect. When compassion is real, there will always be action that follows compassion.

A third truth that pictures the fullness of God's forgiveness for all prodigals is the father's love. Verse 20, *...and fell on his neck, and kissed him...* Here is the boy who has the stench of the pigsty on him, but he gets a smooch from the parent in grand style. That is the father's love. God loves sinners. God loves straying saints too. God never gives up on

When Senselessness Gets Sensible

them. God never writes them off. God never says, "You've gone too far." God always cares for them and always has concern for them. I think about the verse that is tucked away in the Old Testament that says that God is married to the backslider. One would think that God would want a divorce; that God would contact an attorney or have a pre-nuptial. No, a thousand times no! God is married. He is there connected to those who are backslidden. In verse 20, the prodigal is broken, burdened, and he is going to be blessed. What does the father do when he sees him broken and burdened? The father goes over and gives him a great big kiss. That is exactly what the father did. The father did not just do it for him, but the Father does it for every single prodigal who wants to get right. There is the kiss of forgiveness. There is the kiss of grace. There is the kiss of mercy. There is the kiss of love because God never gives up on those who wipe out. Truths that picture the fullness of God's forgiveness for all prodigals are the father's looking, the father's longing, and the father's loving.

    I read recently the story of Wrong Way Riegels. On New Year's Day 1929, Georgia Tech played UCLA in the Rose Bowl. Roy Riegels recovered a fumble from UCLA. Picking up the ball, he lost his direction and ran sixty-five yards toward the wrong goal. One of his teammates ran him down and tackled him just before he scored for the opposing team. At half-time, Riegels sat down in the corner and put his face in his hands. Coach Price looked at the team and said, "Men, the same team that played the first half will start the second half." The team started out but Riegels did not move. Coach Price went over to him. Riegels looked up, his cheeks wet with tears. "Coach," he said, "I can't do it. I can't start. I can't go out there. I can't go to the field. I've ruined you. I've ruined the university. I've ruined myself. I can't face that crowd out there."

    Coach Price reached out, put his hands on Roy's shoulder and said, "Roy, it's just half-time. We got the rest of the game yet."

    When we blow it and mess up, when we make a wreck out of our lives, there is a God in glory Who reaches down and puts His hands on our shoulders and says, "Son, Daughter, it's only half-time. We've got a whole other half to play. It's not over yet. The fat lady hasn't sung.

"Give Me That Old-Time Religion!"

There's still a lot of game to go." Then we will recall that the Father has a pardon.

III. The Father Has a Place

Verse 19 says, *And am no more worthy to be called thy son: make me as one of thy hired servants.* The thing that always happens when the foolish Christian becomes wise is that he recognizes the Father has a place. The son's idea was that his dad not recognize him as a son. He would be willing to change his name. The son said to himself, "I won't even keep your name. You don't even have to claim me. You can write me off. You can disown me. In fact, I'll be a hired servant." That was the son's idea. The father interrupts him. His idea is there in verse 22, *...put a ring on his hand...* God always has a better idea. When the son got that ring, he was given a place of service. In Bible times and in Bible lands, whoever had the ring of the family, a signet ring or a family crest ring, could do business for the family. When the father had the servants put that ring upon his hand what he was saying to him is that he may have blown it but there is still a place for him to serve. Just think about the people who God used to write our King James Bible. Moses was a murderer, and God used him to write our King James Bible. Peter cussed, quit, and denied Jesus. He was used to write some of the New Testament. I am not condoning murder. I am not saying someone can go kill somebody, and God will use him. I am illustrating the fact that God has a place for people and that God still wants to use them. When a Christian gets right with God, He just may use them to teach a Sunday school class. When a Christian gets right with God, He just may use him to sing in the choir. When a Christian gets right with God, He just may use him to lead a lost soul to Jesus. The Bible says in Acts 2:14, *But Peter, standing up with the eleven, lifted up his voice.* The swearing Simon has become the preaching Peter. How will God use him? God will use him there on the day when the church is empowered. God will use him on the greatest day of the history of the early church. In one service, after one Bible message, there were three thousand people saved, baptized, and added to the church. Who preached that sermon? Who preached on Pentecost? Who set the precedent and gave us the model of what

When Senselessness Gets Sensible

church ought to be like in the New Testament? It is the preaching Peter who was the swearing Simon! When senselessness gets sensible, we recognize the father has a place.

Richard Wallace, Jr., is the son of Dr. Richard Wallace, Sr. Dr. Wallace pastors a great church in Flower Mound, Texas, a suburb of Dallas. Dr. Wallace is a very faithful pastor and a really very famous preacher and tremendous pulpiteer. When I was preaching there one time, Dr. Wallace picked me up at the Dallas airport. Before he took me out to eat, I could just tell that he was burdened, and between the airport and the restaurant, and the restaurant and the motel that Saturday night, he said, "Dr. Hamblin, would you pray with me about something. My son Richard, Jr., is backslidden. He's away from God, and it's the burden of my heart, and of my wife's heart." He said, "Every day we pray for him. Every day we ask God to bring him back. Every day we pray that the Lord would speak to his heart. He's away from Jesus." He said, "I don't mean to add something to your prayer list. I know there's a lot of names and a lot of needs. I'm sure that people are asking you all the time to put something on your prayer list, but every once in awhile if you could pray for my son, I'd appreciate it."

I said, "Dr. Wallace, his name will go on my prayer list when I get to the motel tonight, and I will pray for him on a regular basis." I said, "Let me say this and if you would please carry it back to your dear wife, your son being backslidden doesn't mean that you failed. If that's the case then we would have to point an accusatory finger in the face of God because Adam and Eve failed." I said, "Dr. Wallace, you stay faithful and true. Tell your wife to stay faithful and true because you know what, there's going to come a time in Richard, Jr.'s life where he's going to need a mom and dad right with God that he can come back to."

Several years passed, and one day my phone rang. It was Dr. Wallace. He said, "Doc, I just wanted to call and tell you we've had an answer to prayer. Richard, Jr., has gotten right." I rejoiced with the brother. We shouted it out. We had our own personal camp meeting over the telephone. He told me about Richard, Jr., getting right with God. A few months passed and he called me again. He said, "Doc, we're

"Give Me That Old-Time Religion!"

starting a Reformers Unanimous ministry here at Temple, and my son Richard wants it."

I said, "Man, that's great."

He said, "He's going to head it up."

I said, "Man, that is awesome."

A couple months passed and he called me and said, "Doc, you're not going to believe this. Temple Baptist Church has a lot of great ministries, but the ministry that brings more people to Jesus than any other ministry in our church is Reformers Unanimous."

I said, "By the way, doesn't Richard, Jr., head that up?"

With much emotion, he said, "Yes, sir, yes sir, he does."

About 3 weeks ago early on a Sunday morning, I got a text message. It was from Richard Wallace, Jr. The text message said, "Doc, you preach like a wild man. I'm praying for you. Let 'em have it, Doc. I'm praying for ya. By the way, today, I'm going to have the privilege of baptizing my son who just recently got saved. And, in the service tonight I'm going to preach. My dad's having me preach, and the church is going to ordain me for the Gospel ministry."

I texted him back and said, "Richard, how many did you have in RU on Friday?"

He said, "Dr. Hamblin, we had 88 in RU."

I texted him back, "That's wonderful. What is your high for RU?"

He texted back, "210."

I said all that to say this, there is a place for every person. God wants to use us. God wants to bless us. We may have made a wreck out of our lives, but there is a God Who is still looking to fix wrecks. He wants to use us in a grand and great way. I think it would be the best if senselessness all of a sudden got sensible, if stupid all of a sudden got smart, if dumb all of a sudden got a degree.

Chapter Twelve

Soulwinning 101

John 4:1-6 says, *When therefore the Lord knew how the Pharisees had heard that Jesus made and baptized more disciples than John, (Though Jesus himself baptized not, but his disciples,) He left Judaea, and departed again into Galilee. And he must needs go through Samaria. Then cometh he to a city of Samaria, which is called Sychar, near to the parcel of ground that Jacob gave to his son Joseph. Now Jacob's well was there. Jesus therefore, being wearied with his journey, sat thus on the well: and it was about the sixth hour.*

For the Christian to graduate from the college of personal work, they must have taken certain core classes. No one ever gets a cap, gown, or a diploma from any school of higher learning because they simply took elective sessions. From the select pages of the Scriptures, a believer not only gets to enroll in the school of evangelism but also gets to be educated on how he can excel in evangelism—*Soulwinning* 101. In John Chapter 4, we find the wonderful conversion of the woman of Samaria. This chapter can be easily outlined or laid out like this:

Verses 1-26 - The Hankering
Verses 27-42 - The Hunger
Verses 43-54 - The Health

"Give Me That Old-Time Religion!"

It is while the Apostle John is under the direct inspiration of the Holy Spirit with the hankering that a believer takes his seat in the class of Soulwinning to be taught by the Master Soulwinner the essentials that will make him an effective soulwinner. John 4:6 says, *Now Jacob's well was there. Jesus therefore, being wearied with his journey, sat thus on the well: and it was about the sixth hour.* Evangelist Oliver B. Greene once wrote this statement about our text: "Let each of us study this account, restudy it, and then study it again, and pray that God gives us patience, wisdom, compassion, mercy, and love, such as Jesus demonstrated here insofar as is possible for us to possess these qualities in Him." Then Oliver B. Greene tied up his thought by writing, "By this example we can become effective soulwinners." Mark it down. To excel in evangelism, it is essential for the saint to be educated by the Saviour. Do not miss that statement. It ever bears repeating. To excel in evangelism it is essential for the saint to be educated by the Saviour. Friend, those of us who are saved will become effective soulwinners as soon as we sign up for the Saviour's soulwinning sessions. Now there are three lessons found in John Chapter 4 that a believer is taught in the Lord Jesus Christ's basic evangelism class—*Soulwinning* 101.

I. The Conversation

John 4:7 says, *There cometh a woman of Samaria to draw water: Jesus saith unto her, Give me to drink.* A key lesson a believer is taught in the Lord Jesus Christ's basic evangelism class is the conversation. In verse 7, the Apostle John tells us about the dialogue the Son of God and the Samaritan woman exchange. For a person to even come close to understanding the magnitude of what is taking place in this scene, he must understand that in this segment of time, the maxim of Jewish society was to never speak to a woman in the street, even if she be thy wife. Burn the words of the law rather than teach them to a woman. Consequently, the four simple words *give me to drink* will result in a wicked person and a wide populace all coming to know the free, full, and forever pardon of sin. Thus, the truth is conveyed by the thought we often cannot have a great conversion until we have had a gentle

Soulwinning 101

conversation. Friend, we will become effective soulwinners when we learn about the conversation.

The Bible says in I Peter 3:15, *But sanctify the Lord God in your hearts: and be ready always to give an answer to every man that asketh you a reason of the hope that is in you with meekness and fear.* It is the Christian who has taken Christ's soulwinning class who knows every conversation and occupation can be turned towards Him. That means when we talk to an architect, we can tell him about the Chief Cornerstone (Ephesians 2:20). When we talk to a baker, we can tell him about the Bread of Life (John 6:35). When we talk to a composer, we can tell him about the One Who can give him songs in the night (Job 35:10). When we talk to a dry cleaner, we can tell him about the One Who will one day render the church without spot or wrinkle (Ephesians 5:27). When we talk to an electrician, we can tell him about the Light of the World (John 8:12). When we talk to a florist, we can tell him about the Rose of Sharon (Song of Solomon 2:1). When we talk to a geologist, we can tell him about the Stone cut out without hands (Daniel 2:34). When we talk to a hobo, we can tell him about the One Who did not have a place or a pillow to lay His head (Matthew 8:20). When we talk to an inebriated individual, we can tell him about the One Who gives non-alcoholic good wine (John 2:10). When we talk to a janitor, we can tell him about the One Who, after a mammoth meal, never leaves fragments (John 6:12). When we talk to a king, we can tell him about the King of Kings (I Timothy 6:15). When we talk to a lord, we can tell him about the Lord of Lords (I Timothy 6:15). When we talk to a midget, we can tell him about the One Who knows the first name of every person who is little of stature (Luke 19:3). When we talk to a newspaper reporter, we can tell him about the One Who, just by the rumor of His presence, would cause the place to be filled by the press (Mark 2:4). When we talk to an octogenarian, we can tell him about the Ancient of Days (Daniel 7:9). When we talk to a pope, we can tell him about the true Mediator (I Timothy 2:5). When we talk to a quack, we can tell him about the One Who healed them all (Matthew 12:15). When we talk to a realtor, we can tell him about the One Who's Father owns many mansions (John 14:2). When we talk to a sinner, we can tell him about the One Who saves sinners (I Timothy

"Give Me That Old-Time Religion!"

1:15). When we talk to a teacher, we can tell him about the One Who taught with authority (Matthew 7:29). When we talk to an uncommitted person, we can tell him about the One Who steadfastly set His face to Jerusalem (Luke 9:51). When we talk to a villain, we can tell him about the One Who wants to take him to Paradise (Luke 23:43). When we talk to a willfully wicked woman, we can tell her about the One Who, if she will come to Him, will say, *Neither do I condemn thee: go, and sin no more* (John 8:11). When we talk to an X-ray technician, we can tell him about the One Who knows his heart (Matthew 15:16). When we talk to a youngster, we can tell him about the One Who is never too busy for little children (Mark 10:14). When we talk to a zealot, we can tell him about the One Who will return to this earth riding on a white horse, leading the cavalry of Heaven, and wearing upon His head many crowns (Revelation 19:11-12). Every conversation and occupation can be turned toward Jesus.

Several years ago, I had the privilege of preaching at the great Temple Baptist Church of Flower Mound, Texas, the home church of Dr. Carl Hatch. If a person was to look up the word *soulwinner* in the fundamental dictionary, right next to it would be the picture of the man whom I call "The Legend," Carl Hatch. A staff member told me about the privilege he had of making some hospital calls with Dr. Hatch. They got inside an elevator at this medical center. There were about ten people in that elevator. Just as soon as the door closed, a lady sniffed and said, "That is wonderful men's cologne. Whose men's cologne is that, and what's the name of it?"

Quicker than it takes to tell the story, Dr. Hatch pulled out his soulwinner's New Testament and said, "That is *Eternity*. Are you ready?" Before the elevator could get to the top floor of that medical center, he had taken his soulwinner's New Testament and led all ten people to the saving knowledge of the Lord Jesus Christ. Dr. Hatch knows that there cannot be a conversion until first there is a conversation.

Someone may say, "I don't like the way Carl Hatch witnesses."

My reply would be, "I like the way he witnesses better than the way you DON'T witness."

It is amazing that those who throw stones at soulwinners are never, never, never soulwinners themselves!

II. The Confrontation

John 4:15 says, *The woman saith unto him, Sir, give me this water, that I thirst not, neither come hither to draw.* A key lesson a believer is taught in the Lord Jesus Christ's basic evangelism class is the confrontation. In verse 15, the Apostle John tells us that before the Samaritan woman can even take a sip of this Living Water, she must have a showdown with the Living Word. No sinner ever gets saved unless he runs right into the Saviour.

> *No sinner ever gets saved unless he runs right into the Saviour.*

F. P. Myer, another great Bible student, once wrote about this verse, "This woman must judge her past sins in the light of those pure eyes, ere she could know the bliss of the fountain opened within the soul." Friend, we will become effective soulwinners when we learn about the confrontation between the sinner and the Saviour.

Before there ever was a sinner, there was a Saviour. There were some things that Jesus had to make clear to this individual before she could be converted. The truths that the Lord Jesus Christ caused the Samaritan woman to see before she ever got saved are the same facts that the soulwinner must cause the sinner to see before he can be saved.

First of all, there is the recognition of her desperate need. John 4:16 says, *Jesus saith unto her, Go, call thy husband, and come hither.* Now according to our narrative, this dear lady had been married five times. She cannot be saved, born again, or have her sins forgiven until there is the recognition of her desperate need. It is not until one sees the real wickedness of his sins that he can sense the real worth of his Saviour.

A second truth that the Lord Jesus Christ caused the Samaritan woman to see before she was ever saved is the recognition of her denominational nonsense. John 4:20 says, *Our fathers worshipped in this*

"Give Me That Old-Time Religion!"

mountain; and ye say, that in Jerusalem is the place where men ought to worship. Before we can even start to think about finding the right place of worship, we better think about finding the right One to worship. We do not go to Heaven because we are Baptist. We go to Heaven because we are born again. Billy Sunday said that the largest caverns in Hell will be filled with church members. Before we figure out where to worship, we should find out Who we are supposed to worship; and that is Jesus.

The third truth that the Lord Jesus Christ caused the Samaritan woman to see before she was ever saved is the recognition of His deity. John 4:26 says, *Jesus saith unto her, I that speak unto thee am he.* It is only Christ that can be omnipotent. One must realize the truths that the Lord Jesus Christ caused the Samaritan woman to see before she was ever saved are the same facts that the soulwinner must cause the sinner to sense before he can be saved: the recognition of her desperate need, the recognition of her denominational nonsense, and the recognition of His deity noticed.

In the Roman gallery of the British museum, there is a long line of marble busts erected on pedestals bearing the names of emperors from long ago. These are of intense interest, for they enable the visitor to look upon the likenesses of Roman emperors who, for weal or woe, held in their hands the destinies of the world. An earlier bust of Nero shows a nature at work, a complexion less coarse, and the brutal elements less pronounced. There is still an inclination, though fugitive, towards better things. In a latter bust however, we see written for us with indelible marks, the change pronounced upon a human countenance by unbridled passion and unchecked cruelty. In the interval between those two busts, Nero had murdered his mother, set Rome on fire, and burned the Christian to appease the populace. We see in his brutal face, his heavy eye, his sensual lips, and thick neck the marks of the beast that he had become. When one looks at their own personal sculptor on the pages of the written voice of God, he stares at the verbal description of his desperate need. He stares at his likeness on the pages of the written voice of God.

III. The Continuation

John 4:29, *Come, see a man, which told me all things that ever I did: is not this the Christ?* A key lesson a believer is taught in the Lord Jesus Christ's basic evangelism class is the continuation. In verse 29, the Apostle John tells us that in the moments after the Samaritan woman was saved she became a significant soulwinner. An individual must pay close attention to the fact that her first activity as a babe in Christ was to leave what she once thought was eternal, which was really temporal, to go to those people she knew with what she thought was temporal, which she now knows is eternal. Verse 28 says, *The woman then left her waterpot, and went her way into the city, and saith to the men.*

J. Hudson Taylor, the great missionary, once said, "Some are jealous to be the successor to the apostles. I'd rather be the successor of the Samaritan woman who, while they went for food, forgot her water pot in her zeal for souls." This female, without taking a new convert's class, filling out a tithing envelope, or posing pretty for the church's pictorial directory, gets nearly every man in her city to come to Christ. Friend, we will become effective soulwinners when we learn about the continuation.

The Bible says in Proverbs 11:30, *The fruit of the righteous is a tree of life; and he that winneth souls is wise.* Proverbs 11:30 means exactly that. Our hyper-Calvinist acquaintances try to jerk, misrepresent, and twist Proverbs 11:30. They do the same thing with John 3:16. They go on this long diatribe that John 3:16 does not mean what John 3:16 mentions. Some Christians think that they were brought to the Living Water only to study it, sit around and sing about it, and even figure out how they might be able to sell it. We were given Living Water, so we might give out Living Water.

Billy Sunday's choir director, Mr. Homer Rodeheaver, told the following touching story about a boy who sang in his choir:

"Joey was not quite right. He would never leave the tabernacle at night until he could shake my hand. He would stand right next to me until the last man had gone in order to say goodbye. It was embarrassing at times. One evening a man came forward to speak to me."

"I want to thank you for being so kind to Joey," he said. "He isn't quite right, and he's never had anything he enjoyed so much as coming here to sing in the choir. He's worked hard during the day in order to be ready to come. It's through him that my wife and I and five children have been led to the Lord. His seventy-five year old grandfather, who has been an infidel all his life, and his grandmother came tonight. Now, the whole family is converted."

Oh, that God would grant us ten thousand not-that-bright Christians in our fundamental churches! Then they could bring one million new converts into the family of God in just twelve months. God give us people not quite that bright who are soulwinners.

We have seen from the pages of the Bible the basic soulwinning instructions every saint needs. I think all of us will see better results when we get back to the rudiments. The greatest soulwinners are always those who have been trained by the Son of God. Would you like to enroll? Would you like to get in the class? Sign up to take Jesus' soulwinning class.

Chapter Thirteen

The Person in the Shadows from the Story of the Prodigal Son

Luke 15:11-19 says, *And he said, A certain man had two sons: And the younger of them said to his father, Father, give me the portion of goods that falleth to me. And he divided unto them his living. And not many days after the younger son gathered all together, and took his journey into a far country, and there wasted his substance with riotous living. And when he had spent all, there arose a mighty famine in that land; and he began to be in want. And he went and joined himself to a citizen of that country; and he sent him into his fields to feed swine. And he would fain have filled his belly with the husks that the swine did eat: and no man gave unto him. And when he came to himself, he said, How many hired servants of my father's have bread enough and to spare, and I perish with hunger! I will arise and go to my father, and will say unto him, Father, I have sinned against heaven, and before thee, And am no more worthy to be called thy son: make me as one of thy hired servants.*

Verse 17 again, *And when he came to himself, he said, How many hired servants of my father's have bread enough and to spare, and I perish with hunger!* I wish everyone would place a mental tent around the word, *servants*. Sometimes, in the light of the brightest Bible truths, there lies other great thoughts in the background of those same brilliant

"Give Me That Old-Time Religion!"

Bible truths. In Luke Chapter 15, we find the tragedy of being lost. This chapter can be easily outlined or laid out like this:

>Verses 1-7 - The Lost Sheep
>Verses 8-10 - The Lost Shekel
>Verses 11-32 - The Lost Son

It is while the physician Luke is dealing under the direct inspiration of the Holy Spirit with the lost son that a person is wonderfully introduced to an unknown and unnoticed individual in this powerful narrative. Preachers have devoted and delivered countless messages, and rightfully so, on the prodigal son, the father, and the elder brother. I think that someone needs to call the church's attention to the servant. The servant is mentioned four times within the span of twenty-two verses. He is mentioned for the first time in verse 17: *And when he came to himself, he said, How many hired servants of my father's have bread enough and to spare, and I perish with hunger!* Do not let that word *hired* throw us off. I Peter 1:18-19 says, *Forasmuch as ye know that ye were not redeemed with corruptible things, as silver and gold, from your vain conversation received by tradition from your fathers; But with the precious blood of Christ, as of a lamb without blemish and without spot.* Just as that servant was bought, every born again servant of God has been bought and paid for by the blood of the Crucified One. Again, the first time we find the word *servants* or *servant* is in verse 17. The second time is in verse 19: *And am no more worthy to be called thy son: make me as one of thy hired servants.* The third time is in verse 22: *But the father said to his servants, Bring forth the best robe, and put it on him; and put a ring on his hand, and shoes on his feet.* The fourth and last time we find the word *servants* in this narrative is in verse 26: *And he called one of the servants, and asked what these things meant.* In the span of some twenty-two verses, we find the word, *servants,* being used four different times.

Now again, we have heard about the prodigal son, the father, and the elder brother; but friend, we need to discover the other cast member that performs on the stage of the lost son. That other cast member is none other than the servant. Now I am not saying that a fundamental preacher, a Bible believing preacher, and a good man of God has never preached on this topic; but it has been my experience that in over a quarter of a century of being saved and in the service of the Lord, I have yet to hear an entire message, from start to stop, on the subject of the servant. I believe that he is that person in the shadows from the story of the prodigal.

Now let us notice three characteristics of the father's servant. If we are saved, we need to be the Father's servant. My, we would have revival! We would have a revival that would go down in the history books of Heaven. We would have a revival that would make the headlines of Heaven if our churches could find some servants; not just saved people, but some servants. Some people whose lives would mirror the life of those servants in Luke Chapter 15. Let us notice the person in the shadows from the story of the prodigal!

> *We would have a revival that would make the headlines of Heaven if our churches could find some servants; not just saved people, but some servants.*

I. Their Provision

Verse 17, *How many hired servants of my father's have bread enough and to spare, and I perish with hunger!* A true characteristic of a father's servant is his provision. In Luke Chapter 15, the physician Luke tells us about how the prodigal had come to himself. Because the prodigal was under conviction, he came to himself in a pigpen in a far away country. The Spirit of God was working and moving in his life. There in that pigpen, he has a revival meeting. The Bible says that he comes to himself, and he thinks back to his father's farm. He thinks back about those who work for his father and he makes the statement, "Why the hired servants of my father's have bread enough to spare, and here I perish with hunger!"

A characteristic of a father's servant is his provision. The deli sandwiches are much thicker and tastier at the father's house than they are at the far country. In the far country, this lad ate things that

"Give Me That Old-Time Religion!"

were against his Jewish diet, the Old Testament, and the oracles of God. However, back at the father's house, there is always good meat, good meals; and the meat and meals of the father's house never violate the oracles of God.

The Bible says in Psalm 37:25 *...yet have I not seen the righteous forsaken, nor his seed begging bread.* That was an old man's testimony. That was the testimony of the sweet Psalmist of Israel. Before he says, "Goodbye" to this world and "Hello" to another world, he says *...yet have I not seen the righteous forsaken, nor his seed begging bread.*

I was preaching at a revival meeting in Pikeville, Kentucky, when a man approached me after the service one night. He said, "Dr. Hamblin, I've got question. I believe that you might have the answer."

I said, "Sir, if I don't have the answer, I'll do my best to get you the answer."

I could just tell by his demeanor and his attitude that it was a sincere question. I have all the time in the world for people who have sincere questions. I have all the time in the world for people who may not understand a truth or understand a thought that is in the Bible. However, as soon as I pick up on my spiritual radar that they are being a smart aleck or they just are not interested in the truth, I have a Bible admonition that I am not supposed to *take of the pearls of truth and cast them before lost swine.* As long as someone is serious and sincere in their seeking of truth, I have all the time in the world for them. I am more than happy to answer any question. I think sometimes Christians waste valuable time on people that are only interested in being smart alecks and smarty pants. If a person is sincere and seeking truth, then I have time for him.

I could just pick up on my spiritual radar that this individual had a good heart and was interested in truth and was not trying to be a smart aleck. He said, "You know, I have marked in my Bible the verse that David said, *I have been young, and now am old; yet have I not seen the righteous forsaken, nor his seed begging bread.* I've got that in my Bible." He turned to it and showed it to me. He said, "But I've got a question. Luke 16:21 says, *And desiring to be fed with the crumbs which fell from the rich man's table: moreover the dogs came and licked his sores.* I know

The Person in the Shadows

there are no contradictions in the Bible, but Dr. Hamblin, I have to be honest with you. For years, those two verses have plagued me. For years those two verses have just been absolutely heavy upon my mind. I don't understand."

I said, "Well sir, you've got to keep reading in Luke Chapter 16. You can't stop at one verse. You have to keep reading in that narrative. You have to keep reading in that story. You have to keep reading in that account, because it's not very long on the other side of the door in eternity that the entire scene changes and the entire scene switches. Now it's not the rich man that has everything; it is Lazarus that has everything. It's not Lazarus that is begging for crumbs; it is the rich man begging for water."

When one is a servant of God, he may not have filet mignon all the time. He may have mac and cheese and peanut butter and crackers. I would rather have mac and cheese and peanut butter and crackers in the will of God than to have filet mignon out of the will of God. We need to see a characteristic of a true servant, not just somebody that is saved, but somebody that is saved, and a servant is his provision.

There have been times since I have been saved that there has been more month than money. If I said that it has not been tight, I would not be telling the truth. However, there has never been a time that I have gone without a meal. There has always been food in the cupboard. Maybe it is not as much as I thought ought to be there, but there has been stuff there.

When one is a servant of God, God will make sure that he gets breakfast, lunch, and dinner. I cannot figure it out or explain it. I cannot give the recipe; but if one is a servant of God, there will come provisions from God. One may say, "Well, I just couldn't live from hand to mouth." I feel sorry for Christians who do not live from hand to mouth—God's hand to their mouth. There is nothing more exciting than to not have it and wonder from where it is going to come and watch it get there. There is nothing more exciting than that. There is nothing more exciting than to have a bill come in the mail and realize that there is no money to pay it. It is a wonderful thing to watch the bill come, and in less than twenty-four short hours, watch God show up and take care of it. I am not just

"Give Me That Old-Time Religion!"

talking about for saved people, but I am talking especially for those who are saved and are servants.

I read a story about a drunkard who was converted, and some of his friends were mocking and making fun of him. These so-called friends found him in the lunch hour reading about the miracle of the loaves and the fishes, and about Jesus turning the water into wine. As he was reading those great miracles, some of his former friends began to mock him and make fun of him and say, "You say you're a Christian. You used to party and carry on with us. You used to go to all the haunts of Hell with us, but now you're too good for us. Now you read your Bible during the lunch break and memorize verses. Now you have quit telling dirty jokes. You tell us about how Jesus turned the water into wine. Have you ever seen Jesus do that?"

The former drunkard thought for a moment as tears welled up in his eyes, and he said, "No, no. I'm sorry. I can't tell you I've ever seen Jesus turn water into wine." (By the way, let me add that this man was sold out to the Saviour.) He said, "No, I've not seen Jesus turn water into wine; but I've watched Jesus take my paycheck and turn it into shoes for my daughter, a dress for my wife, and food for my family instead of it going to liquor, gambling, or the Devil." He said, "I've watched where that's happened! Hallelujah!" A true characteristic of a servant is his provision.

II. Their Project

Luke 15:22 states, *But the father said to his servants, Bring forth the best robe, and put it on him; and put a ring on his hand, and shoes on his feet.* A true characteristic of a father's servant is his project. In verse 22, the prodigal gets home. Before he had the stink of the pigpen off of him, he had the silk of the home place on him. Upon his arrival, there was a party, a parade, a ball, a big time, a jubilee, a jamboree that took place here. The son just started to head home, and the father started to head for the son. In verse 22, the boy is back and immediately the father sends out his footmen to retrieve some things for the found son.

There is some activity that goes on here. There are some people who are busy. Yes, there is shouting and rejoicing going on; but wait a minute. In the midst of the shouting and rejoicing, in the midst of the big time, there is work involved. There is much hustle and bustle. Here are these footmen of the father. These men are going here and there and doing this and that. Though it is a time of blessing, it is also a time when work must be done to make that blessing even bigger.

A true father's servant has a project. We were not saved just to look good or fill some position. We were not saved just to have our name on the church roll or to sign a Bible. We were saved to serve; and as a servant of the Father, there is work to be done! We have a project, and we are supposed to carry things from the Father as His footman to the found son.

> *We were saved to serve; and as a servant of the Father, there is work to be done!*

First of all, notice that an item that was requested by the father for the footman to retrieve for the found son was the robe. This speaks of acceptance. Now to really get the full impact of it, go back to Genesis 41:41-42. In these verses, Pharaoh and Joseph have a conversation; and Joseph is advanced because he is a child of God.

One's attitude always determines his altitude. If we have a good attitude in the world, God will bless us. If we have a good attitude in the church, God will bless us. If we are trying to do over and above what a Christian should do, God will do for us what He did for Joseph, Daniel, and countless other Bible characters. Our attitude there determines our altitude. We drag into work five minutes late, moan, groan, and belly ache about everything the boss asks us to do. We read our Bible when we ought to be working for the man. I am not impressed with what truth we think God gives us when we are shirking the man. I do not want anyone to tell me about what God gave him when he should have been on the job. I do not believe God gave him anything. He just stumbled upon something. I know Christians who want to talk about the Bible and be witnessing when they ought to be working. They do not give their employer a full day's work for a full day's wage. They are a blight for the cause of Christ and are an offense to Jesus. It is a good Christian that works when he is on the job. It is a good Christian that

"Give Me That Old-Time Religion!"

honors what the man asks him to do. It is a good Christian that works for his employer and has a good attitude. One's attitude will there determine his altitude.

Joseph achieves an advancement. The Bible says in those two verses in the Old Testament, that Pharaoh gives Joseph a silk robe. That silk robe was a mark or a measuring stick of Pharaoh's acceptance of Joseph. It is amazing that in Luke Chapter 15, the son gets a robe as well. When does he get it? He gets it as soon as he gets back.

That is not all; secondly, there is the ring that speaks of authority. In Genesis 41:41-42, Pharaoh took off his ring and presented it to Joseph. In Bible times and lands, those of means and monetary greatness usually had either a signet ring or a family crest ring. Whoever possessed the ring could do business for the family. As soon as the prodigal returns, the father sends the servant to go get the ring that speaks of authority.

I am glad when we get right with God, God will give us something to do. Maybe we will not be able to do what we once did, but there is something that we can do. We can get the ring back. God has a job for us even if we have blown it. Now, I have to preface that because if one is out robbing banks and gets right with God, He will give him something to do; but we are not going to give him the ring of the offering plate. We will make sure he gets a ring and will find him something to do. I do not understand Christians who say, "Well, I'm too good to work in the nursery." Mrs. Hamblin had a female Bible college student say to her, "Well, I just don't do nursery." She said, "You will do nursery, and you'll do nursery whistling 'Victory in Jesus'!" Oh, Jesus died on the cross for us. He shed His blood for us and laid down His life for us. He rose again from the dead for us, and we do not do nursery?

There is nothing that we should not be willing to do for the Lord Jesus Christ. This attitude of, "Well, I don't do nursery. I don't do junior church, and I don't do the bus ministry." It is not what we pick; it is what God picks for us.

It is good to start in those places that nobody else wants to start in because those are the places that God will bless. If we do not want the Devil to attack us, we should not surrender to preach, marry a preacher, or work in the bus ministry. Then the Devil will leave us alone because

The Person in the Shadows

every one of those is a front-line ministry. If we do get in a front-line ministry, God will bless us if we are faithful. God will use us and honor our work if we are faithful. Those jobs that nobody else wants ought to be the jobs, tasks, and responsibilities that Christians strive to do because not everybody is clawing and clamoring for those positions.

I can remember when I went into evangelism. Everybody told evangelist jokes. However, after thirty years, everybody wants to be one. They are lining up to say, "Well, how do you become an evangelist?" One should find out what God wants him to do, get in that place, and be faithful; and God will bless. Then everybody will want to be what he is doing. Then everybody will want to jump in and be a part of what he is doing, which is a good thing. A person should find out what the Father wants him to do and give himself to it with all his heart, might, and soul.

Then thirdly, there were the regal shoes. This speaks of affluence. The Bible is a book of divine detail. In Bible times and lands, people wore sandals. Therefore, if Luke 15 says it was a shoe, then it was a shoe. It was not a sandal that was supposed to say shoe. Those who had shoes were those of great wealth. This speaks of affluence.

When we got saved, God made us somebody. God thought so much of us that He bankrupted Heaven that we might be saved. When we wander out in the far country or when we get right with God and come back, the shoes are still there. God still thinks a great deal of us. He still loves us, and we can put those shoes right back on because they speak of affluence.

In Luke 15:22, the Bible says, *But the father said to his servants, Bring forth...* and *put it on him...* Here is the project of the footman of the father. The father knew something about human nature, the nature of his son. If the father would have said, "Now we're glad that you're back, and we're glad that you got right with me. We're thrilled that you're here; but you know that we've got cows to milk, chickens to feed, and pastures to plow. We'd love to spend time with you, but we're busy. Though we're glad you're back, we're busy. What you need to do is go back to your closet. In the back, there is a dry cleaning bag with the best robe in it. You get it, and you put it on." That is not what the Bible says.

"Give Me That Old-Time Religion!"

The Bible says that the father said to the servants, *...Bring forth...and put it on him...* The father knew the nature of man and the nature of his son; and he knew if he would have just said, "Hey, you know where the robe is. We're busy with farm work, and we don't have time for you. You go get that robe. God bless you! We're glad you're back! We appreciate it." If he would have done that, the father knew that the robe would have never gone back on the boy. What does the father do? The father sends a servant for the job. A servant is what we do not want to be. He sent a servant, and what does the servant do? The servant goes and gets the robe and puts the robe on the prodigal. He does not even hand it to him, or he may drop it. He did not put it at his feet; because if he would have put it at his feet, he would have never picked it up. However, the father knew the nature of man and the nature of his son. Hence, he has the servant put the robe on him. That is what we ought to be doing. We ought to be putting robes on people. When we do, we are a servant. It does not stop there.

Look at verse 22 concerning the ring. If the father would have known that the son would put the ring on, he would have said, "Son, go get the ring." However, the father knew the son would never have gone and gotten the ring. In fact, for the longest time I did not understand why the son gives this apology speech. Right in the midst of it, the father cuts him off. All of a sudden, it seems like the father ignores him. For the longest time, I thought, "Man, that's rude." Here this boy is trying to get right, and the father just absolutely cuts him off. He starts calling for things and demanding things to be carried to his son because actions speak louder than words. The boy was back so there was no need for a speech or a press conference. There was no need for a statement. Forgiveness is there because actions speak louder than words.

There are some husbands and wives that have a memory like an elephant. Every time he or she does something the other does not like, he or she will go into the grave of the past and dig something up and stick it in front of him and say, "You said this and did that." I am glad that God is not like that. He sends the servant to get the ring. Those that have a memory like an elephant concerning past wrongs and offenses had better pray to God that they never mess up. If we have that kind

The Person in the Shadows

> *Those that have a memory like an elephant concerning past wrongs and offenses had better pray to God that they never mess up.*

of attitude, we are going to mess up. We will reap a whirlwind of people putting before us things that God has forgiven and forgotten.

The father sends the servant to get the ring. The father knew about the nature of the son. He knew if he would have said, "Man, we're glad you're back, but we're busy. There's a field to plow, cows to milk, and chickens to feed. We're glad that you're back, but we can't mess with you. We have stuff to do. Go get the ring." The father knew he would not have gotten it. Hence, he sent the servant to get the ring. The servant puts the ring on the finger. The servant did that because the father knew that the prodigal would have never gotten it put on.

We Christians are just the same. We get away from the Lord and miss a service or two. As we are driving to Sunday school or an evening service, we go to turn our blinker on to pull into that church parking lot. As we hit that blinker to turn, suddenly the Devil says, "What do you think you're doing? You missed a service or two. If that wasn't bad enough, when you missed a service or two, you went to a rock concert, a bar, and a tattoo party. What are you doing going to church?" Just before we turn that wheel, we say, "I can't go there because I've been out in the far country. I can't go to the Father's house." We have all been there. We have gotten out of the will of God, and as soon as we go to pick up our Bible, old Smutty-face, Lucifer, Beelzebub with bad breath slides up next to us and says, "What are you doing? You're picking up that Bible. Why you're picking that Bible up with the same hand that you put in a rock and roll CD into your CD player. What are you doing? You're picking up that Bible with the same hand that you picked up a beer." The Devil says, "What are you doing turning those Bible pages. Look at your fingers; they are stained with nicotine. What are you doing?" That is when somebody needs a servant. This is when somebody in the parking lot sees that car getting ready to turn in, but then turns back. That is when somebody needs a servant to run out and say, "Wait a minute. Hold it.

"Give Me That Old-Time Religion!"

You are welcomed here. We're glad you're here." Put the robe on! When they have their fingers stained with nicotine is when they come back. They are trying to hide it. They are trying to put it in their pocket to cover it up. That is when they need somebody to just shake their hand or hug their neck and say, "You know what? God bless you! I was there. I was there, but the Lord helped me. I fell back a couple times, but the Lord helped me. You know what? The same Lord that helped me is the Lord that wants to help you." What we are doing is putting a robe and a ring on somebody. It does not stop there.

There are those regal shoes. The father said to the servant, "Put shoes on him too." The only way we can put shoes on somebody is for us to get down. They do not have to get down, but we have got to get down. They can remain standing in an upright position, but we have to get down to get shoes for the prodigal. When we give someone the regal shoes, we have to get down and humble ourselves. We have to realize, only by the grace of God, that could be us.

I get really nervous when I get around Christians and hear about faults and flaws of others. They act as though they do not have any faults or flaws of their own. I get really uncomfortable when I am around people that are constantly feeding other people into the verbal paper shredder. I am thinking, "If they are doing that while I'm here, what are they doing when I'm not here?"

Someone may ask, "Well, how do we put regal shoes on people?" The prodigal is going to get back and get the robe and the ring. Nevertheless, before we can even get him the regal shoes, he is going to say, "I really blew it. I made a mess of my testimony. I got out in the world, and I don't know what I was thinking. Things I would have never thought I would have ever done are the things that I did. I can't believe I got a robe. I can't believe I got a ring." That is when we servants are going to show up.

The prodigal is going to show up for visitation because we are going to invite him. He is going to reach into that regal robe and find those Gospel tracts. He is going to pull out a Gospel tract and is going to go give it to someone. Right in mid-pass, he is going to stop and act like he has been shot. He will put it in his pocket because he is going to think

The Person in the Shadows

about what he did out there in the far country. That is when we need to get down and make sure those shoes are on. We can encourage him by saying, "Pass out that tract. I know you blew it. I know that you did some things for which you're sorry. Go ahead and pull that tract back out of your pocket; and give that message to somebody because God wants to use you."

I am so sick and tired of the attitude that is so prevalent in our fundamental churches. We do not realize where we could have been, where we could have gone, or what could have happened to us. The only difference between the prodigal and the servant is the grace of the Father. That is the only difference. Since that is the only thing that is the difference, I want to encourage the prodigal. Maybe one day the prodigal will be the servant for me when I become the prodigal. The servants have a project. They have something that they can do.

> *The only difference between the prodigal and the servant is the grace of the Father.*

III. Their Perception

Luke 15:26-27 says, *And he called one of the servants, and asked what these things meant. And he said unto him, Thy brother is come...* A characteristic from Luke 15 of a father's servant is his perception. However, the elder brother was a prodigal too. The elder brother was just a prodigal who stayed home. The younger brother was a prodigal who left home. When the elder brother finds out that his brother has come back, he goes to the servant and asks, "What is going on? What is the meaning of all this rejoicing? What is all this noise that is drifting from the father's house? What is all this celebration? What is going on?" Here is a son that should have been a servant asking a servant what the father was doing for a son. It is the father's servant that has the perception. If we want to know what is going on at the father's house, just find a father's servant. They will know what is going on in the father's house because they have the perception.

A number of years ago before the "Preach It From the Housetop" tent meeting, someone sent a flyer to Channel 7 News. A reporter from the news station called the pastor early in the week and asked if it would

"Give Me That Old-Time Religion!"

be all right if he sent out a camera crew and a reporter. He wanted to get some information about the annual tent meeting. The pastor agreed. Thus, they sent out a reporter and a camera crew. Before the service, they pulled the pastor and me aside and interviewed us extensively. Before they ever turned a camera or a microphone on, we were very careful in saying, "You need to tell us what you are going to ask us when you turn on the camera and a microphone is in front of us." They were very gracious and cooperative. They said, "We just want to interview you. We got a flyer about this great annual tent meeting of this church. We like human interest stories, and we think there's a story here that our viewers would want to find out about. That's why we're here."

We were both comfortable with that, so they turned on the camera and put a microphone before both of us and interviewed us extensively. When they finished with the two interviews, they asked us, "Would it be all right if we stayed and just filmed the service?" Of course, we both said, "Yes, that would be great!" We figured they would not stay for two sermons. There is just no way. We are talking about a lost camera man and a lost reporter. We switched the order, and I preached first. When the first part of the service was over, someone heard the reporter say to the camera man, "We've got both interviews from Dr. Mendez and Dr. Hamblin. I think we've got enough coverage of the tent meeting and the first preacher. We just need to go ahead and go. We're through here." The camera man said, "You can go if you want to, but I want to stay and hear the whole thing." Consequently, the reporter and camera man stayed for another preaching service. When they left there, they had their hearts filled with truth and their pockets full of Gospel literature.

About three weeks later on the six o'clock news on Channel 7, a ten-minute report aired that I could not have written. The coverage of that tent meeting showed preaching on Hell and people getting saved and right with God. It had the fingerprint of God all over it. When you want to know what is going on at the father's house, go to a servant because he has perception.

Chapter Fourteen

My Name is Stephanas and I am an Addict

I Corinthians 16:15 says, *I beseech you, brethren, (ye know the house of Stephanas, that it is the firstfruits of Achaia, and that they have addicted themselves to the ministry of the saints.)* There is in this verse a name and a verb that I wish to place a mental tent around. The name is *Stephanas*, and the verb is *addicted*. My subject is, *My Name is Stephanas, and I'm an addict*.

The major problem of the complacency in the church could be resolved in twenty-four short hours if only there were a considerable number of Stephanas saints. Just as the chemical junkie is driven by a temporal fix, the spiritual junkie is driven by an eternal fix. The moment that the believer gets hooked upon Heaven's pharmaceuticals will be the same moment that believer moves to a higher plain of spiritual happiness. "My name is Stephanas, and I'm an addict." In I Corinthians Chapter 16, we find the Apostle Paul's final counsel. This chapter can be easily outlined or laid out like this:

Verses 1-4 - Paul's Collection
Verses 5-9 - Paul's Commitment
Verses 10-20 - Paul's Coworkers
Verses 21-24 - Paul's Closing Words

"Give Me That Old-Time Religion!"

It is while the Apostle Paul is dealing under the direct inspiration of the Holy Spirit with Paul's closing words that a person is wonderfully introduced to a worthy individual. Verse 15 states, *I beseech you, brethren, (ye know the house of Stephanas, that it is the firstfruits of Achaia, and that they have addicted themselves to the ministry of the saints.)* The male believer, Stephanas, was one of the first believers in Achaia. His name means "crown-bearer." There are only three times in this Epistle, and for that matter, in the entire New Testament, that he is listed. The first time is in I Corinthians 1:16. The second time is in I Corinthians 16:15. The third and last time that we find Stephanas in Paul's Epistle to the Corinthians is in I Corinthians 16:17. The word *addicted* that is associated with his name, means "devoted by a customary practice." Never forget the Bible snapshot of brother Stephanas should be the exact same Bible snapshot of every saint in the entire family of God. Do not miss that statement. It even bears repeating. The Bible snapshot of brother Stephanas should be the exact same snapshot of every saint, believer, and child of God in the family of God. Friend, those of us who are saved should be addicted, just like Stephanas.

Now, we have a problem. Our problem is complacency. It seems as if complacency just hangs over the heart of the child of God and hovers over the house of God. Although that may be our problem, I am glad we have a solution. The solution is for those who are saved to be just like Stephanas, addicted, not to the passing, but to the permanent; addicted, not to the temporal, but to the eternal; addicted, not to the meaningless, but to the meaningful. There are three tremendous things that those of us who are saved need to have a total addiction toward.

I. Preaching God's Word

Matthew 3:1-2 says, *In those days came John the Baptist, preaching in the wilderness of Judaea, And saying, Repent ye: for the kingdom of heaven is at hand.* A tremendous thing that the believer needs to have a total addiction toward is preaching God's Word. In Matthew 3:1-2, the Apostle Matthew tells us how John the Baptist steps out of obscurity to begin his prophesied ministry of preparing the way for the Lord Jesus Christ. It is within those two small verses that an individual learns his

My Name is Stephanas and I am an Addict

God-assigned method, *preaching*; and his God-appointed message, *Repent ye*. One well-known Bible student once said about him, "He (John the Baptist) was a Heaven-sent surgeon who instantly recognized the symptoms of a fatal disease, and proceeded to challenge it with a scalpel called *repentance*." His stirring life-long addiction started with, *In those days came John the Baptist, preaching in the wilderness of Judaea* (Matthew 3:1), and then sadly stopped with, *And his head was brought in a charger, and given to the damsel* (Matthew 14:11). John steps on to the stage of Scripture preaching, and he steps off the stage of Scripture doing the same thing, preaching. Talk about someone who literally preached their head off—that is exactly what John the Baptist did!

Poet Susan Soria captured her devotion in declaring the Word of God well when she picked up the poet's pen and put upon poet's paper, "Just Preach On."

> If you're preaching from the Bible, well, preach on;
> If you're longing for revival, just preach on.
> Preach on sin and condemnation,
> Preach for sinners, His salvation,
> Preach to Christians, consecration—
> > But preach on.
>
> If your sermon's from the Lord, then preach on.
> Never mind if some look bored, just preach on.
> If the Devil looks down on it,
> If the critics frown upon it,
> Many souls depend upon it—
> > So, preach on.
>
> If you step on someone's corns, well, preach on.
> "Take the bull right by the horns," and preach on.
> Even though we may not like it,
> Even though some try to fight it,
> Where there's wrong the Lord can right it—
> > So preach on.

"Give Me That Old-Time Religion!"

Let not time be a restriction, just preach on.
If a sinner's got conviction, then preach on.
Christ can save his soul from Hell,
Cleanse his heart and make him well,
(Even if it's after twelve)—
        Just preach on!

From the Law to Revelation, yes, preach on.
Christ for every situation, oh, preach on!
Even if your members doubt it,
And say they can do without it,
If you've talked to God about it—
        Then preach on!

Think of Christ's own message clear, and preach on.
There for all who wish to hear, oh, preach on.
All are sinners—they must know
That His blood did freely flow;
He can wash them white as snow—
        Oh, preach on.

In the Holy Spirit's power, oh, preach on!
He'll reward you in His hour, just preach on.
Broken hearts and sins forgiven,
Blessings here so freely given,
And a crown up there in Heaven—
        Oh, preach on!

Friend, we need to be addicted to preaching God's Word. The Bible says, in I Corinthians 1:21, *...it pleased God by the foolishness of preaching to save them that believe.* When a believer is a "junkie" on preaching, he looks forward to church days. He will not be distracted, discouraged, or derailed by his detractors. He will "storm the fort" in every service as if it were the last night of a two week revival meeting. I do not understand preachers who say, "Nuts! It's Sunday," or "Rats, it's Wednesday night." I am never discouraged when I preach. I am discouraged when I do not preach. I believe America needs a revival of preaching. I believe America needs a revival of just absolutely raring back, letting her go, letting her fly, and letting her have it!

> *I believe America needs a revival of preaching. I believe America needs a revival of just absolutely raring back, letting her go, letting her fly, and letting her have it!*

I do not understand preachers, who say, "Man, I hate it. It's Sunday. Oh, I hate it. It's Wednesday night." I do not understand preachers who just get distracted, discouraged, and derailed by their detractors. I am not using myself as any kind of an example, but I preach better when somebody is upset in the crowd. When Mrs. Hamblin was with me in a revival meeting just the other day, I said to her, "Babe, if I'm not getting plugged in, if I'm not getting after it, and if it seems like I'm a little slow getting out of the gate, would you sit there and act disgruntled? That would help me." I do not understand preachers who reach the point where they want to jump out of a basement window, overdose on baby aspirin, or slit their wrists with plastic wear, just by a little look or a little word from the crowd. I just do not understand it. I do not understand preachers who just mess around when they get in the pulpit. The high hour of the week is when the man of God, led by the Spirit of God, preaches the Word of God. We need a revival of preaching.

I am not saying that when a preacher preaches, he ought to preach like me. I am not saying that, but it would help if a preacher had a pulse. I read somewhere, maybe it was Greek Mythology, but I read somewhere that I am supposed to earn my bread by the sweat of the brow. Would to God that preachers had a pulse, and preachers had punch! A preacher ought not to preach and give the crowd the impression that rigor mortis has set in. A young man, Dr. Brent Stancil, once wrote a poem to introduce me. He wrote: *Dr. Hamblin is a Great Preacher Without Question.* (Again, I don't agree with that, but I do like to hear it.)

"Give Me That Old-Time Religion!"

> *Dr. Hamblin is a great preacher without question,*
> *But may I make you a very small suggestion?*
> *Do not attempt to preach with the same style or action,*
> *Or else your body will end up in traction!*

Now, I am not saying that when a preacher preaches he ought to preach like me; but what I am saying is there ought to be a punch, a pulse, and a power. There is nothing in America that cannot be resolved and remedied with old-fashioned, red-hot, spirit-filled, Bible preaching.

Charles Spurgeon once spoke about a certain preacher, whose name was Oncken, who was preaching in Hamburg, Germany. This preacher was brought up before the Bürgermeister many times and imprisoned. This magistrate one day said to Mr. Oncken in very bitter terms, "Do you see that little finger?", speaking of his own. "Yes, Sir" came the reply. "As long as that little finger can be held up, Sir, I will put you down." "Ah," said that preacher, "I don't suppose you see what I see. For I discern not merely a little finger, but a great arm. It is the arm of God. As long as that arm can move, Sir, you never, never, never can put me down." Of course, that preacher went right back to what he was addicted to, and that was preaching the Bible. God, give us in our fundamental churches and pulpits more men of God who have joy in their delivery and who have punch in their preaching. Oh, to be addicted to preaching God's Word! Young preachers should not wait for an opportunity to preach, but they should create an opportunity to preach.

II. Praising God's Work

Psalm 22:22 states, *I will declare thy name unto my brethren: in the midst of the congregation will I praise thee.* A tremendous thing the believer needs to have a total addiction towards is praising God's work. In Psalm 22:22, the Psalmist David tells us of his sorrows and sufferings which picture the Lord Jesus Christ's sorrows and sufferings. In the midst of the minor notes of this song, he makes sure to strike the major note by singing in the midst of the congregation *while I praise thee*. By the way, that should answer for time and eternity the question,

My Name is Stephanas and I am an Addict

"Is it all right to praise God in church?" The Bible says, *In the midst of the congregation will I praise thee*. It is in the house of God that we ought to be rejoicing. It is in the house of God that we ought to be praising. It is in the house of God that we ought to raise our hands and shout, "Hallelujah!" It does not bother me how loud someone shouts, how high he jumps, or how far he runs, just as long as he speaks in English when he is doing it! For too long we have allowed those who are in heresy, in false doctrine, and in ignorance of the Bible to steal our shout. It is high time that we take back our shout, our joy, and our rejoicing. How in the world does someone rejoice with heresy? How in the world does someone get happy about false doctrine? How in the world do people who are wrong on the Bible get more excited than those of us who are right in the Bible?

> *It is high time that we take back our shout, our joy, and our rejoicing.*

We ought to be addicted to praising God's work. Some people may say, "Well, it's just so noisy over there in that church." Well, I guess when a person goes to a cemetery church, a God-praising church would seem noisy. They say, "Well it's just so rowdy over there." I think Heaven is going to be noisy. I think Heaven is going to be a little rowdy. When I get to Heaven I just cannot imagine that they are going to pass out the order of service. I could be wrong, but I just cannot imagine that. Christian, this is the quietest world we will ever live in. Church ought to be a forerunner, a foretaste of Heaven.

Some time ago, I was sitting on the platform waiting to preach with the pastor of the church seated next to me. The special music did such a wonderful job that the audience just burst out in applause. The preacher leaned over, and I just knew what he was going to ask me. He leaned over, and he framed it like it was going to be some dark question. He said, "Dr. Hamblin, I have to ask you, does it bother you when people clap in church?" I said, "My brother, I'm happy for any kind of noise. If people burp, as long as it's in the right place, I'm happy about it." Friend, we need to be addicted to praising God's work. When a believer is a

"Give Me That Old-Time Religion!"

"junkie" on praising, they will have a song in their heart, a smile on their face, and a spring in their step.

The first exciting thing that the believer should be shouting over is amazing salvation. Psalm 18:46 says, *The Lord liveth; and blessed be my rock; and let the God of my salvation be exalted.* The Christian would "raise the roof" if they just remembered how great redemption was, is, and forever shall be. I mean, it is just eternal life, everlasting life, life forever; it is just forgiveness forever, that is all it is.

One time, as I was flying to Nashville, I stopped at Starbucks in the Metropolitan Airport. After I got a cup of coffee, I gave the young lady a Gospel tract. I said, "Ma'am let me give you something to read that I wrote. It's from the Bible." This dear black lady said, "You're one of us?" I said, "Well, I'm saved." She said, "Well, I'm saved, too." Then, she high-fived me right there in the Metropolitan Airport. She was excited about it! We ought to be excited about being saved. We ought to be excited that our sins are forgiven. We ought to be excited that we are children of God.

A second exciting thing that the believer should be shouting about is answered supplication. Psalm 28:6 says, *Blessed be the Lord, because he hath heard the voice of my supplications.* The reason some saints do not praise God is that either they forgot about an answer to prayer, or they failed to get an answer to prayer. I appreciate when somebody says, "Hey, let me tell you what God did in way of answered prayer." I never tire or get weary in hearing answers to prayer. That is something that we ought to be shouting about. Maybe the reason our Wednesday night prayer meetings in the average fundamental, independent, Bible-believing, Bible-preaching, pre-millennial, missionary-minded, soulwinning, temperamental Baptist church are so dead is that we do not take a moment to praise God for answered prayer. I am not being harsh, and God knows my heart; but sometimes I get in the place to preach on Wednesday night, and it is just like I am looking for them to roll the casket down the aisle. I am looking for someone to do the committal service. I am looking for someone to just set the headstone. I mean, it is dead. It seems like we get to the Wednesday night service; a starter pistol goes off; and we have got to hurry up and get this done. We have to hurry up and finish this, because kids have to be in bed at eight. Stupid is not written all over my forehead. Do not give me that line, "The kids got to be in bed by eight." They have never been in bed at eight. Church in a red-hot house of God will help them more than all the sleep in the universe. When we put them in bed and cut the service short, what we are saying is that junior and sissy are running the church.

I realize that we have to be conscious of time, but what about the Wednesday night service? Why are we in such a hurry to get it through? What if we just slow the service down a little bit; and before we get to that Bible study, we just take a little time for praise reports. What if on Wednesday night we say, "Now, before we have the Bible study and prayer requests, I wonder, does anybody have a praise report?"

Somebody raises his hand and says, "Yes, I've got a praise report. Last week, I had the preacher and the people pray that I'd get a job. This past week I had somebody call and ask me to work for them; and God answered the prayer of the pastor and of the people; and I got a job."

Then, somebody else raises his hand and says, "You know, I've got a wayward son, or I've got a wayward daughter; and I'd asked the church to pray last Wednesday about it; and out of the blue they called me. They're somewhere in the country, but they went to a fundamental church and got right with God. I just want to praise the Lord, and thank the church for praying." That will revitalize our Wednesday night services. They would be alive and exciting because we took some time for praise reports.

Imagine that I am sitting in a service that is taking praise reports, and I have a prayer request. A lady says, "I just want to praise the Lord. My husband was sick, and I asked the church last Wednesday night to pray for him. God answered the prayer." At this time, I am still waiting to give my prayer request, but they are still taking praise reports. The lady continues by saying, "We've taken him to the doctor, and he's doing a lot better. The doctor can't explain it. God answers prayer."

Now, I am sitting in the service waiting to give my prayer request. I hear her praise report, and I think to myself, "If God can do it for this lady; God can do it for Hamblin, because God doesn't have any favorites. If God did it for her, I don't have to have grey hair for God to answer my prayer. God loves His children. He wants to answer prayer. If He did it for one, He can do it for another."

All of a sudden, Wednesday nights are a revival meeting! Would that be all right? Could we handle that? Would that be okay? I know junior and sissy have to go to bed, but would it be all right if God moved in on Wednesday night? What would change our Wednesday night services is if we just slowed down and said, "I'm going to take a praise report." When the preacher opens it up for a praise report, we ought to have praise on our lips for what God has done for us.

A third exciting thing that the believer ought to be shouting about is abounding satisfaction. Psalm 68:19 says, *Blessed be the Lord, who daily loadeth us with benefits...* The everyday blessings of God should bring about the everyday bragging of believers on their God. Oh, that every believer would realize the exciting things they should be shouting about are amazing salvation, answered supplication, and abounding satisfaction!

One day, a former drunkard was praising God for taking away all of his appetite for liquor. A physician argued with him stating that would have to mean that he had a new stomach in order for him to have his appetite for liquor removed. "Praise God," said the former drunkard, "I always knew that I had a new heart when I got saved, but this is the first time I found out that I got a new stomach, too!" Forgive those of us who are excited about getting saved, because God gave us a new heart, a new stomach, new hands, new feet, and a new home. Forgive us, because we are just rejoicing and reveling in what God has done.

> *Forgive those of us who are excited about getting saved, because God gave us a new heart, a new stomach, new hands, new feet, and a new home.*

III. Presenting God's Way

Acts 16:30-31 says, *And brought them out, and said, Sirs, what must I do to be saved. And they said, Believe on the Lord Jesus Christ, and thou shalt be saved, and thy house.* A tremendous thing the believer needs to have a total addiction toward is presenting God's way. In Acts 16:30-31, the physician Luke tells us of the stirring question of the Philippian jailer and of the scriptural answer of the Apostle Paul and his coworker Silas. Even though Paul and Silas had been bloodied, bruised, and bound, they still were bent on telling the would-be-suicide correction officer, *Believe on the Lord Jesus Christ, and thou shalt be saved, and thy house.* This is an addiction of the most serious sort. Friend, we need to be addicted to presenting God's way. The Bible says, in Romans 1:16, *For I am not ashamed of the gospel of Christ: for it is the power of God unto salvation to every one that believeth; to the Jew first, and also to the Greek.* When a believer is a junkie on presenting the Gospel, they will pass out Gospel tracts all the time, think of unique ways of witnessing, and pray every day that God would make them an outstanding soulwinner.

Several years ago I was checking out of the Comstock Inn after finishing a revival meeting in a church in Michigan. As I was waiting in the lobby for the elevator, I saw a man dressed in a green maintenance man uniform with a white patch with the name "John" in red cursive stitch. He was standing next to me at the elevator. I pulled out of my pocket what every Christian ought to carry on their person at all times—a Gospel tract. If I do not have a Gospel tract on me, I almost feel like I am not dressed. I almost feel like I am not right with God if I do not have a Gospel tract on me. I reached in my pocket, pulled out a Gospel tract, and I said, "Is your name John?"

He said, "Yes."

I said, "What a great name, John. There's a man in the Bible named John. There's a preacher who wrote a Christian classic which has been read more widely than any other book outside of the Bible. His last name was Bunyan, but his first name was John. There's another preacher who was called the twentieth century's mightiest pen. His last name was Rice, and his middle initial is R, but that's not all that important, because his first name was John. My name's John. What a great name!"

He kind of smirked. I handed him that Gospel tract; and just as I handed him the Gospel tract, the lady clerk that was on duty that night

"Give Me That Old-Time Religion!"

craned her neck around the front desk and hollered, "JOHN, BRING THAT TO ME RIGHT NOW!" About that time, the elevator door opened, and I jumped in and pressed the close elevator button. My grandfather, a golden gloves boxer, whom I was named after, taught me "He who fights and runs away lives to fight another day." I really did not want to know what, "JOHN, BRING THAT TO ME RIGHT NOW!" was all about.

So, I rode the elevator to the second floor and went into my room. That week, I was in room 224. I got the luggage cart and put all my luggage on the cart. As I was riding the elevator back down to the lobby, I decided what I was going to do was get out of there as quickly as I could. I was going to go through the lobby, pack my vehicle, and sign out of the room as quickly as I could because I was really not interested in what that, "JOHN, BRING THAT TO ME RIGHT NOW!" was all about.

The elevator door opened; and I got the luggage cart out of the elevator, through that fancy, fine lobby of the Comstock Inn, through the first set of double doors, but had some difficulty with the second set of double doors that led to the parking lot. Just my luck, I got that luggage cart stuck in the second set of double doors. About that time, John comes running towards me. As he drew nearer, I could see tears in his eyes. He got to the second set of double doors where I was standing, laid hold of the luggage cart, and said, "I'm just coming to tell you, John, that I got saved. I just trusted Christ. Thank you for that Gospel tract. I was just born again."

I said, "God bless you, John! That's wonderful. God bless you! Welcome to the family of God, John." I went to check out, and the motel clerk, who said, "JOHN, BRING THAT TO ME RIGHT NOW!" looked at me and said, "I know who you are. You were here about two months ago. When you were checking out, you reached into your pocket, and you pulled out one of those green things that you wrote. You gave it to me, and I got saved. You gave it to me; and I read it; and I trusted Christ." She said, "What you need to know is John's a little deaf, and he can't read. I watched you give him that Gospel tract. I called him over and read it to him, and I led him to Jesus Christ. I just think you ought to know about that."

My Name is Stephanas and I am an Addict

    Oh, listen, that is what I want to be hooked on. That is what I want to be addicted to. That is what I want to be plugged into—presenting God's way. Stephanas was addicted. Not to the passing, but the permanent, not to the temporal, but to the timeless. We have a problem, and our problem is complacency. It hangs over the house of God. It hovers over the heart of the child of God. The solution is for us to be just like Stephanas in that we are to be addicted. What is your name? How about you? Are you addicted?

"Give Me That Old-Time Religion!"

Chapter Fifteen

What My Elijah Taught Me

II Kings 2:9-11 says, *And it came to pass, when they were gone over, that Elijah said unto Elisha, Ask what I shall do for thee, before I be taken away from thee. And Elisha said, I pray thee, let a double portion of thy spirit be upon me. And he said, Thou hast asked a hard thing: nevertheless, if thou see me when I am taken from thee, it shall be so unto thee; but if not, it shall be not so. And it came to pass, as they still went on, and talked, that, behold, there appeared a chariot of fire, and horses of fire, and parted them both asunder; and Elijah went up by a whirlwind into heaven.*

The verse I would like to emphasize is verse 11: *And it came to pass, as they still went on, and talked, that, behold, there appeared a chariot of fire, and horses of fire, and parted them both asunder; and Elijah went up by a whirlwind into heaven.* There are two words in this verse that we should underline, if not in our Bibles, then certainly in our minds. They are the two very small and almost inconspicuous words *and talked*. I would like to convey what my "Elijah," Dr. Tom Malone, Sr., taught me.

Every good servant of God has been instructed by an even greater servant of God. No one has ever climbed to the top of the mountain of spiritual effectiveness without the teaching, tutoring, or training of

"Give Me That Old-Time Religion!"

someone who was already on that same mount. Whatever the capable Christian knows today is solely because of what the considerable Christian had imparted to him yesterday. In II Kings Chapter 2, we find the supernatural translation of Elijah. This chapter can be easily outlined or laid out like this:

>Verses 1-13 - The Companion
>Verses 14-15 - The Spectators
>Verses 16-22 - The Doers
>Verses 23-25 - The Mockers

It is while the unknown writer is dealing under the direct inspiration of the Holy Spirit that a person reads a heart-captivating two-word phrase *and talked.* Verse 11 says, *And it came to pass, as they still went on, and talked, that, behold, there appeared a chariot of fire, and horses of fire, and parted them both asunder; and Elijah went up by a whirlwind into heaven.* The word *talked* in the Hebrew language means "to command or to commune; to teach or to tell." Just on the surface, one would wrongly think that they were just "shooting the breeze," or just "chatting it up." But going beyond the surface, we see in the Hebrew language, this word *talked* has a much deeper meaning than simple idle chatter. This verse seems to indicate that there would never have been a prophet Elisha if it had not been for the influence, instructing, and impact of the prophet Elijah.

A Bible student of another century once wrote about our text: "Elijah so fully matured that he was ready for translation, side by side with Elisha who was just blossoming out in the beauty of early faith and devotion." The sister verse of II Kings 2:11 is Jeremiah 5:5. There, the Bible says, *I will get me unto the great men, and will speak unto them; for they have known the way of the LORD, and the judgment of their God...* No one will ever sit at our feet to be trained until we first sit at someone else's feet to be taught. Do not miss this thought. It even bears repeating. No one will sit at our feet to be trained until we first sit at someone else's feet to be taught. Friend, those of us who are saved need to remember what our older spiritual fathers have relayed to our ears. I want to give three outstanding truths on which my Elijah instructed me.

I. Scripture is Primary

II Timothy 2:15 says, *Study to shew thyself approved unto God, a workman that needeth not to be ashamed, rightly dividing the word of truth.* A truth that my Elijah instructed me on is that Scripture is primary. II Timothy 2:15 states that the way the believer knows the approval of God is by being very acquainted with the Word of God. We will not know the approval of God until we know the Book of God. This verse that was penned to a young preacher not only speaks to him but also speaks to every person in the family of God that they are to know the Book. We are to know the Scriptures. We are to know the Bible. We are to know the written voice of God. An unknown poet must have had this thought upon his heart, when he picked up his pen and wrote this heart-penetrating poem:

> Down in the wood-clad hills,
> All somber and stately and old,
> Men go to burrow in the ground,
> To seek for gems of gold
>
> I burrowed in a richer bed;
> I struck a richer ore
> Of gems of gold that never fail,
> That last forevermore.
>
> I mined deep down within God's Word
> Where riches all abound;
> God helped me, and my heart rejoiced;
> His gems of gold I found.
>
> And now I want to share with you
> The wonders of my find.

"Give Me That Old-Time Religion!"

Come! Help yourself! This gold is yours,
All ready, all refined.

Friend, we need to remember what my Elijah taught me—Scripture is primary. The Bible says, in Proverbs 23:12, *Apply thine heart unto instruction, and thine ears to the words of knowledge.* Newsflash: No Christian will ever hear an "Amen!" from Heaven in regards to their life when every time a preacher preaches from the Gospel of John he turns to the maps section in his Bible trying to find it. Hey, if we are to know the approval of God, we have to go to the Book of God. If we are going to be used of God, if we are going to have the hand of God upon us, then we have to know the Book of God. I believe it is an absolute tragedy that there are people that have been saved for decades who have absolutely no clue about anything in the Bible. They carry it upside down or sideways. Some of them do not even carry it at all because they absolutely have no knowledge of the Bible.

Right after I got saved, in September of 1979, I had the wonderful privilege of preaching for the first time with Dr. Tom Malone, Sr. It was within sixty short days of being saved and God calling me to preach. Little did I know, as a young preacher, that after that service Dr. Malone would pull me close and begin to personally mentor me as a man of God. For the twenty-seven years that followed, he and I shared pulpits, motel rooms, platforms, automobiles, airplanes, classrooms, board meetings, basketball courts, and restaurant tables. I am glad and grateful to have his spiritual fingerprint upon me. I am glad to have his spiritual DNA upon me.

One day, I gave him my preaching Bible and asked him to write on the blank pages between the Old and the New Testaments and to give me words of advice for my entire ministry. On March 1, 2002, my Elijah wrote five great truths. I will not list all of them, for some of them are too precious to share publicly, but I will dare to list two of them. The first thing he wrote from soul to ink was about the Word of God. He wrote: *This Book you cannot hold in your hand only, it must be held with the heart.* He underlined the word *heart*. Then, he wrote number two: *Fill this Bible with many great, spirit-filled sermons. Study this book for your own heart and the sermons will come to your own heart and to your own soul.* What my Elijah was saying to me was, "Make sure that in your life as a Christian and in your ministry as a preacher, the Bible is always foremost." Scripture is primary.

II. Separation is Paramount

Genesis 1:4 says, *And God saw the light, that it was good: and God divided the light from the darkness.* A second truth that my Elijah instructed me on is that separation is paramount. Now the word *paramount* means "most important." In Genesis 1:4, Moses tells us that within the first few hours of creation of this blue marble called earth, God makes a difference between the light and the darkness. He does this by dividing them. Another word for *divide* is the almost forgotten word among Christians and Churches, the word *separate*. Mark it down that a person is not even five verses deep in the first book of the Bible when they see that God is commanding old-fashioned separation. Friend, we must remember that what my Elijah taught me is that separation is paramount.

Now, I realize that we live in a day when churches and Christians say separation is not important. But, I am glad that before my Elijah took off to Heaven, he made it crystal clear to me; and I am trying to make it crystal clear to others that separation is paramount. There are several things from which the Biblical doctrine of separation teaches the believer to keep his distance. Keep in mind that the word *divide* means "separate." Separation is not something invented by some cranky or irritable preacher just to give us a hard time. Separation is in the Bible. I know that the flesh does not like it. I know that the Devil does not like it. I know that the world does not like it. I know that backsliders do not like it, but God likes it. It was God's idea, not man's idea.

> *Separation is not something invented by some cranky or irritable preacher just to give us a hard time. Separation is in the Bible.*

"Give Me That Old-Time Religion!"

Looking at the average fundamental, independent, Bible-preaching, Bible-believing, pre-millennial, missionary-minded, soulwinning, temperamental Baptist church, one would not be able to find separation if he hunted for it. I am not talking about lost people, but people who are saved and know better. Church is not the mall or the beach. If we would not wear our church clothes to the beach, then why would we wear our beach clothes to the church? I do not have church clothes and non-church clothes. All my clothes I can wear to the house of God, even my flannel pajamas. They are more modest than what some people wear to the house of God! I think we have lost our minds when it comes to separation. Again, I am not talking about lost people who do not know any better; I am talking about saved people who have been saved for a while.

Now listen, if someone has just trusted the Lord Jesus Christ, we will give him grace and space; but if someone has been saved for a while, he needs to find out that separation is in the Bible. Separation is not the preacher's idea but God's idea. It is high time that people who have been saved for a while realize that we are in the house of God and we ought to dress like it.

There are several things from which the Biblical doctrine of separation teaches the believer to distance himself. First of all, he should distance himself from ungodly people. II Corinthians 6:17 says, *Wherefore come out from among them, and be ye separate, saith the Lord, and touch not the unclean thing; and I will receive you.* It is not the *what* of separation but the *who* of separation over which most Christians stumble. Most of the time, they do not have a problem with the *what*; they have a problem with the *who*. If we stumble at the *who*, we will for sure stumble at the *what*. If we go ahead and take care of the *who*, we will not stumble at the *what*.

Secondly, the believer should distance himself from ungodly practices. I Thessalonians 5:22 says, *Abstain from all appearance of evil.* We will not have to worry about wrong activities if we stay away from wrong appearances. How many times does a rebellious Christian say, "I know it's not right. I know it doesn't look good, but what's so wrong

What My Elijah Taught Me

with it?" He just answered his own question. If it looks bad, do not do it! A person does not have to be a rocket scientist to figure that out.

Thirdly, the believer should distance himself from ungodly partnerships. II Corinthians 6:14 says, *Be ye not unequally yoked together with unbelievers: for what fellowship hath righteousness with unrighteousness? and what communion hath light with darkness?* It does not matter if it is a secular or sacred task. The Christian has no business holding hands with one of the Devil's children. That is why a Christian should not be a member of organizations such as the Masonic Lodge, civic organizations, or secret societies, and clubs. The only thing I am a member of is a fundamental, independent, Bible-believing, Bible-preaching, pre-millennial, missionary-minded, soulwinning, temperamental Baptist Church. Oh, that every single believer would realize that the Bible teaches us to distance ourselves from ungodly people, ungodly practices, and ungodly partnerships!

I can vividly recall, after preaching with Dr. Malone in one of our annual preaching seminars at a Bible College in Michigan, a certain conversation we had in his office. As we were discussing the meeting, he said, "John, we have to fight in our fellowship the weakness of hobnobbing with the wrong crowd." Then, he went back to discussing the preaching seminar, without missing a beat. Hey, child of God, did you happen to catch what my Elijah was telling me? He was proclaiming to get into a spiritual brawl with anyone and everyone who wants to run with the wrong crowd. My Elijah taught me that separation is paramount.

III. Soulwinning is priority

Proverbs 11:30 says, *The fruit of the righteous is a tree of life; and he that winneth souls is wise.* A third truth that my Elijah instructed me on is that soulwinning is priority. In Proverbs 11:30, the wise man, Solomon, tells us that genuine wisdom is not found in books but in bringing sinners into a right standing with God. If the believer had no other verse in the Bible but this one, it would be enough to teach them that witnessing, evangelism, and soulwinning are to be the task, the thrust, and the thrill of the Christian and the Church.

"Give Me That Old-Time Religion!"

By the way, I would not be a member of a church that was not a soulwinning church. I would not be a member of a church that did not have old-fashioned invitations. I would not be a member of a church that did not have a soulwinning program. If the church has a soulwinning program, we ought to get involved, be a part of it, and do everything we can to keep people out of Hell. Soulwinning is to be our emphasis, our enterprise, and our energy. D. L. Moody used to say that if he had to win a thousand souls in order to make sure of Heaven himself, he would certainly choose to risk it by personal soulwinning rather than to attempt it by public preaching without personal soulwinning. Friend, we need to remember that my Elijah taught me that soulwinning is priority.

The Bible says in Luke 14:23, *And the lord said unto the servant, Go out into the highways and hedges, and compel them to come in, that my house may be filled.* The only way that Heaven gets bigger, the church gets larger, and the Lamb's Book of Life gets thicker is by confrontational witnessing. That is the only way. I love Luke 14:23 because it says if we go, we will grow. It says if we go out to the highways and hedges, the house will be filled. A going church is a growing church. We grow by going soulwinning. If we are not growing, it is because we are not going. If we are not going, we will not be growing. I love that verse because it says if we go, God will fill the house!

Dr. Malone and I had taken a flight from Nashville to Detroit. After landing in Detroit, we flagged down a skycap with a cart to take us to the baggage and pick-up area. As soon as Dr. Malone sat in the front seat with this man, he began to speak to him about his never-dying and ever-living soul. I felt bad because there was no one on the second row of seats for me to even talk to. We had not gone very far when another skycap with a woman stopped and asked if we could drop her off first at her gate because she was running late for a flight to Paris. Just as we started off again, Dr. Malone began witnessing to the driver of the cart. He pressed him with the claims of the Gospel, with the Truth, and with the sweet story of God's redeeming love. I tried to speak to the woman right next to me, but I quickly learned that she did not speak a word of English. Every little bit, Dr. Malone would look back at me to see

What My Elijah Taught Me

how I was doing and smirk. He had heard the woman very clearly say, "Parlez vous francais?" Here we are going through the concourse of the McNamara Terminal at Detroit Metropolitan Airport, and Dr. Malone is quoting Romans 3:23, Romans 5:8, Romans 6:23, and Romans 10:9-10. All I could say was, "French toast, croissant, and French fries!"

Soulwinning is priority! Hey, child of God, my Elijah was saying to me no matter where we are, or where we may be, we need to keep people out of Hell. Christian, keep giving the Gospel. Keep giving the Good News. Soulwinning has to be the *zenith* of our life. He was teaching me something. He was not just saying it; he was showing it. Some of the greatest truths we will ever learn come not from someone teaching us but from the way they live their life.

> *Some of the greatest truths we will ever learn come not from someone teaching us but from the way they live their life.*

On the first anniversary of Dr. Malone's homegoing, Mrs. Malone sent me one of Dr. Malone's suits. She said, "I know my husband would want you to have this." She gave to me a charcoal gray pinstriped suit, a red tie, and a set of silver and royal blue cufflinks. When I got back to my room that night, I looked at the suit and remembered buying that suit for Dr. Malone. I do not know if Mrs. Malone remembers that, but I bought him that suit.

Now I wonder, "What has your Elijah taught you?" Here is the problem we have. We want to be an Elijah. The simple fact that we *want* to be an Elijah does not mean that we will *be* an Elijah. We want people to sit at our feet and learn, but we are not willing to be taught. I can see this fact by the way people sit in the services. I can see this fact by private conversations. I can see this fact in people's attitude towards other men of God. They just think that those preachers are common, ordinary people. By that, we are saying strongly that we want to be an Elijah. If there were not an Elijah, there never would have been an Elisha.

Some may say, "I have not had the privilege of traveling with Evangelist Billy Kelly. I have not had the privilege like you of preaching

"Give Me That Old-Time Religion!"

with Dr. Malone, having meals with him, riding on airplanes, and spending time in his office. I haven't had that privilege." God has given each one of us an Elijah that is just as much an Elijah as Tom Malone, Sr. God has given us an Elijah every Sunday morning, Sunday evening, and midweek service. However, we come to church lazy and indifferent. We do not care. We do not "give a rip." We are going to stand and give an account before God for not listening to the Elijah that God placed in our lives and not being taught what we could have been taught. Every Christian has an Elijah. The questions we need to be asking are, "Are we listening? Are we looking? and Are we learning?"

Chapter Sixteen

The Synagogue of Satan

Revelation 2:8-11 says, *And unto the angel of the church in Smyrna write; These things saith the first and the last, which was dead, and is alive; I know thy works, and tribulation, and poverty, (but thou art rich) and I know the blasphemy of them which say they are Jews, and are not, but are the synagogue of Satan. Fear none of those things which thou shalt suffer: behold, the devil shall cast some of you into prison, that ye may be tried; and ye shall have tribulation ten days: be thou faithful unto death, and I will give thee a crown of life. He that hath an ear, let him hear what the Spirit saith unto the churches; He that overcometh shall not be hurt of the second death.*

A verse I would like to emphasis is verse 9: *I know thy works, and tribulation, and poverty, (but thou art rich) and I know the blasphemy of them which say they are Jews, and are not, but are the synagogue of Satan.* There is in this verse, if my count is correct, a four-word phrase that I wish everyone would place a mental tent around. That phrase is *the synagogue of Satan.*

Some people assume that just because a building has a stained glass window, a steeple on the roof, and a sign on the lawn that says "church," it must be a scriptural assembly. But, in reality, it could be a house of worship that is run and recommended by the Prince of

"Give Me That Old-Time Religion!"

Darkness. If God has His churches on the earth, then the Devil has his churches on the earth as well—the synagogues of Satan. In Revelation 2:8-11, we find the Lord Jesus Christ's message to the local church in Smyrna. This chapter can be easily outlined or laid out like this:

> Verses 8-9a - Wealth in Poverty
> Verse 9b - Fiends in Religion
> Verse 10a - Saints in Persecution
> Verse 10b - Duty in Trial
> Verse 11 - Victory in Death

It is while the Apostle John is dealing under the direct inspiration of the Holy Spirit that a person reads one of the strangest and strongest verses in all of the Word of God: verse 9, *I know thy works, and tribulation, and poverty, (but thou art rich) and I know the blasphemy of them which say they are Jews, and are not, but are the synagogue of Satan.* The sister verse of Revelation 2:9 is Revelation 3:9. There, the Bible says, *Behold, I will make them of the synagogue of Satan, which say they are Jews, and are not, but do lie; behold, I will make them to come and worship before thy feet, and to know that I have loved thee.* Now, it is interesting to note that only two times in the written voice of God do we find the expression *the synagogue of Satan.* The first time is in Revelation 2:9, and the second time is in the sister verse, Revelation 3:9.

Evangelist Oliver B. Greene once wrote about our text: "The Holy Spirit puts no frills or sugar-coating on the words that expose this crooked religious crowd." Now it may come as a surprise or even as a startling thing, but the Bible teaches that Satan has a ministry. Why, he has his ministers (II Corinthians 11:15). He has his doctrines (I Timothy 4:1). He has his synagogues, or churches (Revelation 2:9 and Revelation 3:9). Never forget: Sometimes the synagogue of Satan is either a single religious institution, or it is a system of religious instruction. Do not miss that statement, and it even bears repeating. Sometimes the synagogue of Satan is either a single religious institution, or it is a system of religious instruction. Friend, those of us who are saved need to be able to detect the religious den of the Devil. On our way to church, we will pass many a building, meeting place, and so-called church that are nothing less than synagogues of Satan. Just because there are stained glass windows, a steeple, and a sign does not mean that it is a real, genuine, authentic church. I believe that I have a message that will help every child of God find what is a synagogue of Satan. Let us notice the marks, signs, or indicators of a synagogue of Satan.

I. A House of Worship with Man's Words for Their Scripture

Matthew 4:4 says, *But he answered and said, It is written, Man shall not live by bread alone, but by every word that proceedeth out of the mouth of God.* A sure sign of a synagogue of Satan is a house of worship with man's words for their Scripture. In Matthew 4:4, the Apostle Matthew tells us that when the Devil first tempted the Lord Jesus Christ in the wilderness, it was to try to get Him to turn boulders into bread. Then, the Lord Jesus Christ pulls out his Old Testament personal worker's Bible and puts his finger on Deuteronomy 8:3 and pronounces: *...man doth not live by bread only, but by every word that proceedeth out of the mouth of the LORD doth man live.* From this stirring scene, the Son of God gives us not only the method of success over temptation but also the message of the scriptural church in a turbulent world. Friend, we need to know that a sure sign of a house of worship that is a synagogue of Satan is that they have man's words as their Scripture.

The Bible says in II Timothy 3:16, *All scripture....* I like the beginning of that verse. That word *all* is an interesting word. When we take that word *all* out of the Greek language and put it into the English language, it means "all." *All scripture is given by inspiration of God, and is profitable for doctrine, for reproof, for correction, for instruction in righteousness.* When a church says from their pulpit, platform, or printed material, "*The New World Translation, The Book of Mormon* or the newest translation recommended by the Vatican, Billy Graham, or the World Council of Churches is our Bible," they are not a church but a synagogue of Satan. Now, we have not only an inspired Bible, but also a preserved Bible. It is not just inspired, but preserved from Genesis through Revelation. Every word that is in the Bible is supposed to be in the Bible.

"Give Me That Old-Time Religion!"

I like what Bro. Lester Roloff once said. He said, "We don't need to re-write the Bible; we need to re-read the Bible." We should make no apology whatsoever if we belong to a church that believes that God not only inspired His Word, but also preserved His Word for English-speaking people in the King James Bible. It happens every once in while. People will say to me, "You give the impression when you preach that you are King James only." Congratulations! Move to the front of the class! People say, "We get the inkling that you are King James only." I like to tell those people, "Only if you spell *only* in capital letters." I am glad that we have a Bible. It is not a book of fairy tales. It is not man's reasoning, but God's revelation. It is the Truth.

Some time ago, I read about a middle eastern trader who could not read a word of English, but he kept a King James Bible beside him at all times. He said, "When I meet a trader who is unknown to me, I take the Bible, put it in his way, and then watch him. If he opens it up and reads it, I know that I can trust him. If he throws it aside with a sneer or a curse, I'll have nothing to do with him." Christian, if we want to know if someone is a member or a minister of a synagogue of Satan, then just put a King James Bible in front of him and watch.

II. A House of Worship with Man's Works for Their Salvation

Jude 11 says, *Woe unto them! for they have gone in the way of Cain...* A sure sign of a synagogue of Satan is a house of worship with man's works for their salvation. In Jude 11, the Apostle Jude tells us that ruinous trouble will fall upon the head of every single person who attempts to get to God without going through the required atonement. A well-known Bible student once penned, "The *way of Cain* is basically the rejection of salvation through the blood of a sacrificial victim. It is an attempt to appease God through human efforts."

The Synagogue of Satan

Friend, we need to know that a sure sign of a synagogue of Satan is a house of worship with man's works for their salvation. When a church says from their pulpit, platform or printed material that the only way to Heaven is through the baptistry waters, through rosary beads, confessing one's sins to a priest, taking communion, or going to a stranger's door and having them subscribe to *Awake* magazine, it is not a church but a synagogue of Satan. Mark it down: any plan of salvation that does not have a bloody cross is not a scriptural plan of salvation but a ploy of Satan. We should be glad to be a member of a church that points people to Jesus. We do not point people to works, to water, or to wafers. We point people to Jesus. As a member of a fundamental, independent, Bible-believing, pre-millennial, missionary-minded, soulwinning, temperamental, King James only, Baptist church we should say to people, "Nothing but the blood can wash away our sins!"

Now, there are several tremendous truths that the Bible teaches concerning the blood of Christ. First of all, the blood of Christ is invaluable. I Peter 1:18-19 says, *"Forasmuch as ye know that ye were not redeemed with corruptible things, as silver and gold, from your vain conversation received by tradition from your fathers; But with the precious blood of Christ, as of a lamb without blemish and without spot.* One drop of the blood of the Lord Jesus Christ is more priceless than a thousand Grand Canyons filled with wedges of silver and bars of gold.

Secondly, the blood of Christ is invincible. Revelation 12:11 says, *And they overcame him by the blood of the Lamb, and by the word of their testimony.* The color red must remind the Devil of the defeat he received on Mount Calvary. I am a winner. If we are saved, we are winners. We are winners not because of what is in our pocket, in our bank account, how large our house is, or how expensive our car is; but we are winners because we have been washed in the blood. We have been to the only One Who can give salvation through the crimson flow, and that is Jesus. We are winners. I believe we would have a revival that would make the headlines in the history books in Heaven if God's people would just realize that they are not losers but winners! That ought to infect every part of our attitude. Every person who is saved is a winner. Winners

"Give Me That Old-Time Religion!"

act like winners. They carry themselves like winners. This idea that the Christian is to just mope around and drag their lip on the ground and always be depressed, downcast, and discouraged is absolutely foreign from the Bible. We are winners if we are saved!

Let me try to illustrate. I have always been a Detroit Pistons fan. I am a Piston's fan when they are winning or losing. One cannot be a Pistons fan unless he hates the Chicago Bulls. I have always been a Pistons fan, and I have watched some away games when the Pistons were playing the Bulls in Chicago. I remember when those two teams would get together and play. I would watch those games. It would always inspire me when they called Michael Jordan's name. It always amazed me how the lights would go low; the stadium would grow quiet; and then the announcer would say, "Number 23, Michael Jordan." The stadium went bananas. They went absolutely crazy. The lights would then come on. Michael Jordan would get up off the bench slowly and deliberately, like he owned the place. Though I am not a Bulls fan, I was always inspired by the fact that Michael Jordan would get up on his home court and go out a winner. I am a winner. Those of us who are saved are winners. We ought to act like winners, carry ourselves like winners, look like winners, and behave like winners. This world is not the winning team. Saved fundamentalists are the winning team. We ought to carry ourselves that way.

It is a standing joke in my house that I can get into any hospital no matter what time of day or night. The way that I do is that I do not go to the front desk and say, "I'm here to see so and so. Would you let me in?" No. I walk in like I own the place. I do not ask the head nurse for permission to see anybody. I am on an errand for the King. I just walk in. There has not been one hospital to which I have not been able to get in. I think it has to do with the way I carry myself. I just do what I am there to do.

Would to God that we had some choir members that acted like winners! Would to God that we had some Sunday school teachers that acted like winners! Would to God that we had ushers that acted like winners! I believe that the offerings would increase if we had ushers that acted like winners. Just carry that plate with pride. Just stick it under somebody's nose until they put everything they own in it. We are on the winning team. The blood is invincible. If the blood is invincible, then all those who have been washed in it are winners.

Now, if someone wants to live a discouraged, despondent Christian life, that is his business, but I am not going to be discouraged. If someone wants to wake up every day and say, "Woe is me! I think I'll eat a worm and die." Then go ahead and have two because I am not eating one. We are winners. We ought to act like winners. We ought to carry ourselves like winners. We ought talk like winners. We ought to behave like winners. It is the blood of the Crucified One, the invincible blood that makes us winners.

Thirdly, the blood of Christ is indispensable. Hebrews 9:22 says, *And almost all things are by the law purged with blood; and without shedding of blood is no remission.* The blood is fundamental for the sinner's forgiveness. A person does not get to go to Heaven because he is a Baptist, a Buddhist, or broke. A person gets to go to Heaven because he has been born again. The blood of Jesus Christ has been applied to his soul and to his sin account. The blood of Jesus Christ is indispensable. Oh, that every person would realize the tremendous truths that the Bible teaches concerning the blood of the Lord Jesus Christ are that it is invaluable, invincible, and indispensable.

Sir Arthur Conan Doyle recounts the story of a small detachment of British troops who were surprised by an overwhelming enemy force. The British fell back under heavy fire. Their wounded lay in a precarious position where they faced certain death. One of them, a corporal in the mounted infantry, later told that they realized immediately when they saw the enemy and counted how many enemy soldiers there were and how many able-to-fight soldiers they had, that they needed to come under the protection of the Red Cross flag if they wanted to survive. All they had was a piece of white cloth but no red paint. So, from their wounds they made a large cross on that white cloth. Their attackers respected that grim flag as they held it aloft, and the wounded British were brought to safety. Churches that are recognized by Heaven are those churches that still hold high the blood-stained banner of the

"Give Me That Old-Time Religion!"

> *Churches that are recognized by Heaven are those churches that still hold high the blood-stained banner of the cross, waving it heartily and hollering for all those to come beneath its redemptive color.*

cross, waving it heartily and hollering for all those to come beneath its redemptive color.

III. A House of Worship with Man's Ways for Their Service

II Timothy 2:2 says, *And the things that thou hast heard of me among many witnesses, the same commit thou to faithful men, who shall be able to teach others also.* A sure sign of a synagogue of Satan is a house of worship with man's ways for their service. In II Timothy 2:2, the Apostle Paul tells us that there is to be a sacred passing down of paramount things from the seasoned servants of God to the strong servants of God. An individual gets the mental picture of the aged Paul putting in the hand of youthful Timothy the baton of Truth. The youthful Timothy then takes that baton of Truth and passes it down to those faithful men. Make no mistake about it. It is not just the message. It is the message and the method.

I hear a lot of people say, "Well just as long as we stick with the message, it's going to be all right." Now wait a minute. That is a half-truth. A half-truth is a whole lie. It is not just the message but the method as well. One method we should not change is scriptural worship. We are not tuning in to the TBN crowd to find out how to worship. Paul and Jan Crouch know nothing about Bible worship. We do not tune in to TV to find out about Bible worship. We tune in to the Bible.

Another method we should not change is straightforward preaching. A few months ago I had the privilege of preaching with Dr. Clyde Box, one of my five favorite preachers. We ought to have favorite preachers. Dr. Clyde Box is a great preacher and orator. He paints pictures with words. One night, while we were having a meal together, we were talking about this contemporary craze. Dr. Box looked at me and said, "You know, John, the problem really is not music. We've always had bad music. The problem is we don't have any pulpiteers anymore." Straightforward preaching is a method we had better not change.

The Synagogue of Satan

Another method that we had better not change is soulwinning on street corners, sidewalks, and wherever there is a reachable soul. Personal and ecclesiastical separation is another method that we cannot change. Someone may ask, "What is separation?" Separation is not just yoking up with every donkey that brays a verse of Scripture. At some point in our Christian life we ought to get past the place where just because someone quotes a Bible verse, they must be all right. Separation is more than just quoting a Bible verse. With whom do we run? Who are our associates? What is our agenda?

Someone may say, "Well, where do you find that in the Bible?" The Bible says in Jeremiah 6:16, *Thus saith the LORD, Stand ye in the ways, and see, and ask for the old paths, where is the good way, and walk therein, and ye shall find rest for your souls.* The new way is not of God. It is the old way that is of God. It is amazing that the old way worked for us to be saved, worked for our children to be saved, and worked to keep the church on a parcel of property that is still a bright light in a dark world. I mean, it has worked for all these years! Now, all of a sudden, we know better.

There was a basketball coach that used to say, "If the team is winning, don't change the starters." Profound. I want to go on record as saying that our team is winning. In fact, we are up by ten. We do not need to change the "starters" of scriptural worship, the "starters" of straightforward preaching, the "starters" of ecclesiastical and personal separation, or the "starters" of soulwinning. Hey, our team is up, and we are winning. When a church says from their platform, pulpit or printed material, "We offer a service on Saturday night so that you can get an early tee time on Sunday. At our church, we don't want to make anyone feel uncomfortable by using an antiquated Bible and an ancient hymnbook. If you come hear our Pastor, you'll just love him because you can call him by his first name. When he speaks, he wears casual clothes and doesn't sound anything like a preacher." That is not a church. It is a synagogue of Satan.

We are on the winning team. Our message and methods work. If we belong to a Christ-honoring church, we should thank God that it is not a synagogue of Satan. Let us help our man of God keep it that way!

To Order Additional Copies of

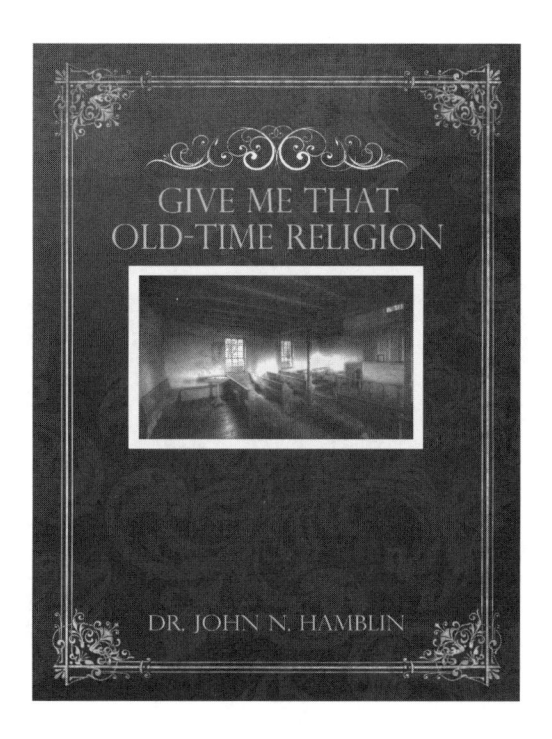

Contact:

BEREAN PUBLICATIONS

4459 US Highway 17
Fleming Island, Florida 32003
Phone: 904-264-5333
Fax: 904-264-9185
Email: info@bereanmail.org
WWW.THEBEREANBAPTISTCHURCH.COM